The Black Watch at Ticonderoga Major Duncan Campbell of Inverawe

Frederick B. Richards

Alpha Editions

This edition published in 2019

ISBN : 9789353299637

Design and Setting By
Alpha Editions
email - alphaedis@gmail.com

30¢

THE
Black Watch
at Ticonderoga
and
Major Duncan Campbell
of Inverawe

By **FREDERICK B. RICHARDS, A. M.**
Secretary of N. Y. State Historical Association : Glens Falls, N. Y.

AN EXCERPT FROM VOLUME X OF THE PROCEEDINGS
OF THE NEW YORK STATE HISTORICAL ASSOCIATION

PRINTED FOR FORT TICONDEROGA MUSEUM LIBRARY

BLA

THE BLACK WATCH AT TICONDEROGA

By FREDERICK B. RICHARDS, A. M., Glens Falls, N. Y

A residence of ten years in Ticonderoga inspired me with an appreciation of the history of that most historic spot in America, and when as secretary of the Ticonderoga Historical Society I was instrumental in securing the erection of the Black Watch Memorial in that village, I became particularly interested in the record of that famous Highland Regiment which this building commemorates.

It has for several years been my wish to write so complete an account of the Black Watch at Ticonderoga that one would need look in no other place for any detail in the history of that regiment from the time it left Scotland in 1756 until after the capture of Ticonderoga by Amherst in 1759. As a meeting of the New York State Historical Association on Lake Champlain seemed an appropriate time to present such a paper and the printed histories of that period give only meagre accounts on this subject, Mrs. Richards and I made this an excuse for a trip to the British Isles and a large part of August and September, 1910, was spent on a Black Watch pilgrimage. We had a very enjoyable trip and gained many interesting facts but I am sorry to say that the story is still far from complete.

The reason for the lack of more detailed information about the Regiment in the Ticonderoga period is found in the following which is copied from the preface of Stewart of Garth's first edition:

"The origin of these Sketches and Military Details was simply this: When the Forty-second regiment was removed from Dublin to Donaghadee in the year 1771, the baggage was sent round by sea. The vessel having it on board was unfortunately driven on shore by a gale of wind, and wrecked; the greater part of the cargo and baggage was lost, and the portion saved, especially the regimental books and records, was much injured. A misfortune some-

what similar occurred, when the army, under the Earl of Moira,
landed at Ostend in June, 1794. The transports were ordered
round to Helvoetsluys, with orders to wait the further movements
of the troops. But the vessels had not been long there, when the
enemy invaded Holland in great force, and, entering Helvoetsluys,
seized on the transports in the harbour. Among the number of
vessels taken were those which had conveyed the Forty-second to
Flanders, having on board every article of regimental baggage,
except the knapsacks with which the officers and soldiers had
landed at Ostend in light marching order. Along with the baggage,
a well-selected library, and, what was more to be regretted, all that
remained of the historical records of the regiment, from the period
of its formation till the year 1793, fell into the hands of the enemy.

"After the conclusion of the late war, his Royal Highness, the
Commander-in-Chief, directed that the Forty-second should draw
up a record of its services and enter it in the regimental books, for
the information of those who should afterwards belong to the
corps. As none of the officers who had served previously to the
loss of the records in 1794 were then in the regiment, some difficulty arose in drawing up the required statement of service; indeed,
to do so correctly was found impossible, as, for a period of fifty-
four years previous to 1793, the materials were very defective. In
this situation, the commanding officer, in the year 1817, requested
me to supply him with a few notices on the subject."

It seemed to have been the custom in the British army of that
period for a Regiment to carry its entire belongings with it from
place to place and this unfortunate practice has swept from existence every trace of the Regimental records of the Black Watch of
Ticonderoga.

It may be readily seen that if Colonel Stewart who had all the
information in 1817 which the British government was able to
supply and who was also fortunate in having had an intimate
acquaintance during his service in the Regiment with officers who
have served almost from its formation, was unable to write a complete record, the task nearly one hundred years later might be
considered well nigh hopeless. There was the hope, however, that
some record which was then lost might have been discovered since
Colonel Stewart's time or that interesting matter might be found in
the archives of the families who had sons in the Black Watch of
1758. It is a fact that only recently the regimental records of the
Black Watch of two decades later were found in an old second-hand

book store in Portsmouth and it is still possible that the regimental records of 1758-9, which are now lost, may yet come to light.

We find that nearly all the histories of the Highland Regiments follow Stewart of Garth nearly word for word in their accounts of the early history of the Black Watch. A notable exception, however, is "A Military History of Perthshire," which has much that is new. There are also many interesting letters and other records in "The Chronicles of the Atholl and Tullibardine Families," relating to the service of those of the Black Watch who came from the Atholl Family or estate, and at London we found some dispatches in the Public Record Office in the War Department which I have not seen published. The chief merit, however, if any, which I can claim for this address is that while it does not add much that is new, it does, I think, collect in one article nearly all that is known about the Black Watch of the Ticonderoga period.

I might say here, also, that whatever was lacking in information was more than made up by the cordiality of our reception, as we found nearly every Scotsman interested in the oldest Highland Regiment of the British Army and glad to help us in any way possible. We are under special obligation, which I here wish to acknowledge, to Lt. Col. Hugh Rose, the present commander of the First Battalion of the Black Watch; Major D. L. Wilson Farquharson, D. S. O., who represented the Regiment at the unveiling of the memorial tablet at Ticonderoga, July 4, 1906, now retired and living in Allargue in Aberdeenshire, the home of the Farquharson's for many generations; W. Skeoch Cumming of Edinburgh, artist and authority on Scottish costumes and tartans of the 18th century; Mrs. Campbell of Dunstaffnage, present owner of old Inverawe House; the Marchioness of Tullibardine, editor of "A Military History of Perthshire," and the Duke of Atholl, present head of the Clan Murray, Honorary Colonel of the Third Battalion of the Black Watch and compiler of the "Chronicles of the Atholl and Tullibardine Families."

Before proceeding to the Black Watch of Ticonderoga, it would perhaps be well to give a brief history of the Regiment. There is considerable difference of opinion as to just when the independent companies which were afterwards to become the present regiment of the line were raised. The earliest record I have seen is that on the 3rd of August, 1667, King Charles II issued a commission under the Great Seal to John, second Earl of Atholl "to raise and keep such a number of men as he should think fit to be a constant guard for securing the peace in the Highlands" and "to watch upon the braes."[1]

From this time until 1739 the Black Watch was in various stages of formation.[2]

It was at the period of the independent companies that the name Black Watch was given—Black from the sombre tartan in contrast to the regular soldiers who at that time had coats, waistcoats and breeches of scarlet cloth, and Watch because their duties were to watch or keep order in the Highlands. The character of the rank and file of the Black Watch of this period was exceedingly high, many gentlemen with servants serving as privates, and in addition to the enlistment being from the best families it was also possible to select only "men of full height, well proportioned and of handsome appearance." There were several reasons for this, the principal one being probably the fact that at that period the carrying of arms was prohibited by penalties and it became an "object of ambition with all the young men of spirit to be admitted even as privates into a service which gave them the privilege of wearing arms." Our interest in the Black Watch, however, is principally in the Regiment of the line as such and this dates from the commission given by George II, October 25, 1739, as follows:

"GEORGE R.—Whereas we have thought fit, that a regiment of foot be forthwith formed under your command, and to consist of ten companies, each to contain one captain, one lieutenant, one ensign, three serjeants, three corporals, two drummers, and one hundred effective private men; which said regiment shall be partly formed out of six Independent Companies of Foot in the Highlands of North Britain, three of which are now commanded by captains, and three by captain-lieutenants. Our will and pleasure therefore is, that one serjeant, one corporal, and fifty private men, be forthwith taken out of the three companies commanded by captains, and ten private men from the three commanded by captain-lieutenants, making one hundred and eighty men, who are to be

---

1 A Military History of Perthshire, Page 28.
2 The most complete account of the independent companies may be found in "A Military History of Perthshire."

GRENADIER, 42ⁿᵈ REGᵗ 1751.
(From a painting at Windsor Castle.)

The tallest men of the Regiment of that period were formed into a Grenadier Company and wore the Grenadier bearskin. The rest of the uniform as above and the substitution of the blue bonnet for the bearskin was the uniform for the rest of the Regiment.

equally distributed into the four companies hereby to be raised; and the three serjeants and three corporals, draughted as aforesaid, to be placed to such of the four companies as you shall judge proper; and the remainder of the non-commissioned officers and private men, wanting to complete them to the above number, to be raised in the Highlands with all possible speed; the men to be natives of that country, and none other to be taken.

This regiment shall commence and take place according to the establishment thereof. And of these our orders and commands, you, and the said three captains, and the three captain-lieutenants commanding at present the six Independent Highland Companies, and all others concerned, are to take notice, and to yield obedience thereunto accordingly.

Given at our Court at St. James's, this 25th day of October, 1739, and in the 13th year of our reign.
By His Majesty's Command,
(Signed) : Wm. Yonge.

To our Right Trusty and Right Well-
Beloved Cousin, John Earl of
Craufurd and Lindsay.

May, 1740, these ten companies were mustered in a field between Taybridge and Aberfeldy and in the army list of that year were known as "Earl of Crawford's Regiment of Foot in the Highlands."[1] There have been several changes of the official name of the Regiment but the "Black Watch" was always the familiar one in the country where it has drawn its recruits and since 1881 has been the official name in the British Army List.[2]

The uniform of this period was a "scarlet jacket and waistcoat, with buff facings and white lace, tartan plaid of twelve yards plaited round the middle of the body, the upper part being fixed on the left shoulder, ready to be thrown loose and wrapped over both shoulders and firelock in rainy weather. At night, the plaid served the purpose of a blanket, and was a sufficient covering for the Highlanders. These were called belted plaids, from being kept tight to the body by a belt, and were worn on guards, reviews, and on all occasions when the men were in full dress. On this belt hung the pistols and dirk when worn. In the barracks, and when not on duty, the little kilt or philibeg was worn, a blue bonnet with

---

[1] See Appendix for list of officers.
[2] See Appendix for the regimental names of the Black Watch at different periods.

a border of white, red, and green, arranged in small squares to resemble, as is said, the fess cheque in the arms of the different branches of the Stewart family, and a tuft of feathers, or sometimes, from economy or necessity, a small piece of black bearskin. The arms were a musket, a bayonet, and a large basket-hilted broadsword. These were furnished by Government; such of the men as chose to supply themselves with pistols and dirks were allowed to carry them, and targets after the fashion of the country. The sword-belt was of black leather, and the cartouch-box was carried in front, supported by a narrow belt round the middle."'[1]

"While the companies acted independently, each commander assumed the tartan of his own Clan. When embodied, no clan having a superior claim to offer an uniform plaid to the whole, and Lord Crawford, the colonel, being a Lowlander, a new pattern was assumed, and which has ever since been known as the 42d, or Black Watch tartan, being distinct from all others.'[2] Lord John Murray gave the Athole tartan for the philibeg. The difference was only a stripe of scarlet, to distinguish it from that of the belted plaid. The pipers wore a red tartan of very bright colours, (of the pattern known by the name of the Stewart or Royal Tartan), so that they could be more clearly seen at a distance. When a band of music was added, plaids of the pipers' pattern were given to them."'[3]

Having given briefly the origin of the Regiment, we will pass to the period which is the subject of our article.

May, 1756, war having been formally declared between France and England, a body of troops, the Highlanders forming a part, were embarked under the command of Lieut. General James Abercrombie and landed at New York, June, 1756. These were soon followed by more troops under the Earl of Loudon who was appointed Commander-in-Chief of the Army of America.

The official name of the Regiment at this time was the 42d Regiment of Foot, but they are often spoken of in dispatches simply as the Highlanders, because they were the only Highland Regiment then in this section, or as Lord John Murray's Highlanders from the custom of the times of calling a Regiment by the

---

1 Stewart of Garth, Page 246, Vol. I.

2 Capt. I. H. Mackay Scoble claims that this tartan was probably evolved from a Campbell Sett and was a Government pattern for Government service, worn by the independent companies of the Black Watch before embodied in 1739 and also by other Scottish regiments. "The Government or Black Watch Tartan" Army Historical Research, Vol. I, Page 154.

3 Stewart of Garth, Page 247, Vol. I.

name of its Honorary Colonel. The commander of the Black
Watch at this time was Lieut. Col. Francis Grant, son of the Laird
of Grant, who had served in the Regiment from the time he had
received his commission as Ensign, October 25, 1739. He was made
Lieutenant Colonel December 17, 1755 and was in command of the
Regiment all through the American campaign. The only other
officer who had served continuously from the formation of the
Regiment in 1739 was Gordon Graham of Drainie, who in 1756 was
senior captain.

The record of the Regiment from the landing in June, 1756,
until the battle of July, 1758, is exceedingly meagre. In fact
nothing of importance was done by the whole army. As one author
puts it "Loudon was so engrossed in schemes for improving the
condition of his men that he seemed to have no time for employing
them against the enemy." The following extract from a letter
from the Earl of Loudon to William Pitt dated New York, March
10th, 1757, will illustrate the method of quartering troops of that
period.

"In the end of your letter you have acquainted me, that words
shall be inserted, in the mutiny act to take away every doubt about
the Right of Quartering extending to America.

When I writ on that subject, I was but just arrived, and the
troops were mostly encamped. Since that I have had disputes to
settle, all over this Continent, in settling the winter quarters for
the Troops from whence I find, that the manner of quartering in
England, as in time of peace, on Publick Houses only, will in no
shape answer the intent in this country, for there are few Publick
Houses and most of them sell nothing but spirits, where they possess
only one room in which they sell the liquor, where men cannot be
quartered.

Whilst the war lasts, necessity will justify exceeding that rule,
as Troops must be under cover, in the places where it is necessary
to post them, for the security of the country and carrying on the
service, but as soon as a peace comes, it will, by the English rule,
be impossible to quarter any number of Troops, in this country,
without a new regulation, and the only remedy that occurs to me at
present, is adopting the method of quartering in Scotland, where
for the same reason of there not being Publick Houses sufficient
for the reception of Troops they are by law quartered on private
houses.

I must beg leave to give you one instance of the situation of quarters here. When I arrived at Albany, I do not believe it was possible to have quartered Fifty men on that town, on all the Publick Houses in it, and taking a full survey of it, I found that by quartering on the Private Houses, I can, without incommoding them, in the parts of their houses, in which they live, quarter Fourteen Hundred men, and for a short time, in case of necessity, I could quarter Two thousand. I have mentioned this to show you what the situation of all the Frontier Places, in this country that are liable to attacks, must be, if quartering is likely to be kept to, on Publick Houses only.

On the 10th instant arrived the Harriet Packet which brought me the duplicates of your letters of the 9th and 11th of January, and the next day came in here His Majesty's ship the Hampshire commanded by Captain Norbury, having under his convoy nine additional companies of the Highlanders,* wha had a passage of twelve weeks from Cork, and met with very bad weather; of this convoy there were missing on his arrival in this Port, the Arundal and Salisbury Transports. The last we have, since, accounts of her getting into Rhode Island.

The Troops being sickly, I have cantooned them in villages adjacent to this Port, for the sake of fresh provisions and vege tables."

In the published histories of the time it is stated that the "42d remained inactive in or near Albany during 1756 and that throughout the winter and spring of the following year the men were drilled and disciplined for bush fighting and markmanship, a species of warfare for which they were well fitted, being for the most part good shots and experts in the management of arms."

From the following letters found in the Public Record Office in London the quarters for the winter of 1756-7 were probably at Schenectady. Extract from letter from Loudon to Pitt, New York, 25th April, 1757, "The Highlanders were set in motion from Schenectady * * * they marched without tents and lay in the woods upon the snow making great fires and I do not find the troops have suffered * * * We have on that River (Mohawk) at Schenectady and up to the German Flats, the Highland Regiment upwards of a thousand men," etc.

---

*3 additional Companies Black Watch and 3 for Montgomery's and 3 for Fraser's, stationed at Halifax.

The second letter reads as follows, and while it is chiefly of interest in this connection because it is dated from Schenectady, it also illustrates the custom of selling commissions:

Schenectady, April 24, 1757.

Francis Grant, Lt. Col. 42d Regiment. Sir:—

I am convinced from several things that have happened me since I have been in the Regiment that my continuing to serve any longer in it would be disagreeable to the whole corps of officers and being likewise sensible of my own unfitness for a military life I have resolved to quit the Army as soon as I can obtain leave to resign my commission. But as I have nothing else in the world to depend upon and finding myself at present at a distance from my family and friends or anyone whom I can depend on for advice, interest or assistance and having frequently experienced your goodness and favor, I have made bold to apply to you that you would be pleased to intercede with his Excellency the Earl of Loudon, in my behalf that His Lordship in consideration of my distressed situation and circumstances might be moved to give me leave to resign in favor of some person that would be willing to allow me wherewithal to support me till I can settle and apply to some other way of life.

In doing me this favor you'll forever oblige, Sir,
Your respectful and gratefully obed't hum. serv't,
George Maclagan, Ens.

P. S.—If it is agreeable to your Lordship I am willing to pay fifty pound Sterling for Mr. Peter Grant Voluntier.
Francis Grant, Lt. Col. 42d. Regt."

With these two dispatches from the British War Office as a clew I have tried to learn more about the winter quarters of the Black Watch and have looked through the Colonial manuscript in the New York State Library, *the Records of the City of Albany and the published works of the period but so far without success. I have been unable to find any Schenectady records of this period. It seems that a valuable collection of Glen-Sanders papers from the old Mansion across the Mohawk from Schenectady was recently sold and I have been told that in these there were several refer-

---

* The only reference to the Black Watch that I could find in the unpublished Colonial Manuscripts in the N. Y. State Library was the report of the receipt at New York, 8th July, 1757, from the ship Free Mason, of 22 Bales, 10 Casks and 1 Box for Lord John Murray's Regiment. Colonial Mss., 1757, Vol. 84, Page 126.

ences to officers of the Black Watch. As the Glens' were Scots it would be quite likely that if this collection were not now scattered to the four winds much information about the Highlanders could be obtained. It is said that Schenectady was only a frontier village in 1756 and not large enough to take care of a regiment and it seems to be a fact from the reference given above that only a part of the thousand men were stationed here as it states that the Regiment was stretched along the Mohawk from Schenectady to the German Flats, but that it was a station for troops is proven by the list in the Public Record Office of the winter quarters for the troops in America for 1758, which states that the Black Watch was quartered in New York and Lt. General Murray's at Schenectady. There is in the Public Record Office no list of winter quarters of the troops in America previous to 1758.*

* After this article had gone to press I received through the kindness of Arthur Doughty Litt, D. Archivist of the Dominion of Canada, a copy of the references to the Black Watch in the archives at Ottawa and one reference proves that the 42nd was stationed at Schenectady the winter of 1756-7, as follows: Nov. 22, 1756, Loudon to Fox, the 42nd Regiment I quartered at Schenectady from whence they take the posts, on the Mohawk River, etc. See Appendix.

It appears, however, from the Town Records of Stamford, Conn., that a committee representing that town made a claim on the "General Court" of the Colony of Connecticut to reimburse them for £369-13-4 1-2 which the town had expended "in taking care of the Highlanders from November 30, 1757, to March 30, 1758. The soldiers numbered 250 officers and men and they had also belonging to them 17 women and 9 children." They were probably part of the Black Watch. The only other Highland regiments of that time were Montgomery's and Fraser's, both raised in 1757 and their arrival at New York from Halifax is noted in the "Post Boy" of April 11, 1757. This town record also further illustrates the custom of that time as previously stated and as an officer of the present Regiment aptly puts it, "they took not only their mess plate but their wives also, on service with them, and sometimes lost both."

1 Col. John Glen, born July 2, 1735, died Sept. 23, 1828, was quartermaster during the French and Indian and also the Revolutionary wars and was a man of great prominence in this locality. His brother, Col. Henry Glen, born July 13, 1739, died January 6, 1814, was deputy quartermaster under his brother and was member of Congress from Albany District from 1794 to 1802. Schenectady at that time was in Albany District. It was Col. John Glen who gave the name to Glens Falls, changing it from Wing's Falls, it is said as the result of a wine supper.

Copy of an old Engraving showing the method of wearing the Belted Plaid

This 250 at Stamford would only be a quarter of the Regiment, however, if Loudon had upwards of a thousand at or near Schenectady the winter before and it is probable that the rest were quartered at or near Schenectady as in 1756.

Another statement that I have tried to confirm is the account by James Grant in his "Legends of the Black Watch" of the 50 chosen men under orders of MacGillivray of Glen Arrow, who went to reinforce Col. Munro at Fort William Henry. It is also said in a foot note of Wilson's Orderly Book that Capt. Gordon Graham was at Fort William Henry at the time of the surrender, and this is repeated in N. Y. Colonial Mss. by O'Callaghan, page 728, Vol. 10, but I have not been able to find any other reference that would substantiate these statements.

The only time the 42d emerges from the haze of mystery from June, 1756, to the spring of 1758, is that they were a part of Loudon's expedition against Louisbourg in 1757, and this was more a summer vacation than an act of war.

If the English could have attacked Louisbourg in the spring or early summer, success would have been certain but Loudon couldn't seem to get started. As a messenger from the Governor of Pennsylvania, who had waited in vain for a reply to a message, said about him he was like "St. George on a tavern sign, always on horse back and never riding on." The expedition did not start from New York until June 20th and entered Halifax harbor the 30th. Even after this delay he was there before Admiral Holbourne, who did not arrive from England with his fleet of 15 ships-of-the-line and 3 frigates, with 5,000 troops until July 10th. Then there was more delay, the 12,000 troops were landed and weeks spent in drilling and planting vegetables for their refreshment. Lord Charles Hay was put under arrest for saying that the "nation's money was spent in sham battles and raising cabbages." The troops were embarked again, but Aug. 4th a sloop came from Newfoundland bringing news of the arrival of three French squadrons at Louisbourg and as an attack after this reinforcement would be hopeless, the costly enterprise was abandoned and Loudon and the troops sailed back to New York where he arrived Aug. 31st. Delay was the ruin of the Louisbourg expedition and drew off British forces from the frontier where they were most needed.

The troops were started immediately up the Hudson as soon as they were landed at New York but Fort William Henry had already been captured Aug. 9th and the French forces had fallen back to Ticonderoga.

The spring of 1758 opened up with bright prospects. Lord Loudon had been recalled and General Abercrombie, with the able assistance of Lord Howe, was in command. Admiral Boscowen was appointed to command the fleet and Major-General Amherst and Brigadier-Generals Wolfe, Townsend and Murray were added to the military staff. Three expeditions were proposed for this year, Louisbourg, Ticonderoga and Crown Point, and Fort Du-Quesne. The army in America had been largely reinforced during the winter and spring. Of these reinforcements the 42d was strengthened by three additional companies and recruits bringing the Regiment up to about 1,300 men.

As we have considerable information about these three companies through the Atholl Records, it will be interesting to turn back and follow them from the start to the beginning of the Ticonderoga campaign. The first item and one of interest because it shows the method of raising companies in those days, is a letter from the Duke of Argyll to the Duke of Atholl, dated London, July 9, 1757.*

"My Lord:—This is to acquaint your Grace that there is to be 3 additional Companies raised for Lord John Murray's Regiment. I believe the nomination of the officers will be left to me and consequently to Your Grace; there will be 3 captains, 6 lieutenants and 3 ensigns and 100 men each company. The raising the men will be the merit of those who shall desire to be officers and if any can be found who have served in Holland, so much the better. Your Grace will have your thought on this but don't promise anybody till you let me hear from you. I shall speak to Lord John but I will bid him consult you and will plainly tell him that the commissions must all be given gratis. The other two Highland Regiments will likewise have the same addition made to them.

I am with the greatest truth and respect, My Lord, Yr Gr's most faithful and obt. h'ble Servant, Argyll

* Atholl Records, page 428, Vol. III.

By the Duke of Atholl's recommendation the three companies were given to James Stewart of Urrard; James Murray, nephew of the Duke of Atholl and son of Lord George Murray; and Thomas Stirling of Ardoch. Three of the new subalterns were from the Atholl estate, namely Lieut. Alexander Menzies and Ensigns Duncan Stewart, son of Derculich, and George Rattray, son of Dalralzion. The three companies were mustered in October and marched from Perth to Glasgow, where they remained until November 15, when they marched to Greenock and embarked December 1st in transports for Cork en route to America.

April 22, 1758, Capt. James Murray wrote from New York to Mr. Murray of Strowan announcing his safe arrival after a voyage of eleven weeks from Cork. The joys of a voyage in those times when it could take ten days to sail from Scotland to Ireland, is illustrated by a letter from Capt. Murray, dated Youghall, 11 Dec., 1757.*

My dear Brother:—This is to let you know that I am just now in good health and safely arrived here with my company. My transport, together with the other five, set sail on the 1st cur't in the evening along with the Convoy; we had a fair wind and good weather until Sunday, early in the morning (when we were past Waterfort in our way to Corck) about eight, there came on one of the most prodigeous storms that the sailors said they had never seen the like before. About two in the afternoon we lost sight of the Convoy and all the transports and have not yet any sure accounts whether they have got all safe into harbours or not. But since I came here I hear that there was five or six ships lost on the Coast that day. The storm abated somewhat Monday morning but it continued bad weather until Friday evening ,during which time we were often in risk of our lives especially twice, once being within two yards of a great rock and the other time when we were on two fathom water going on a sandbank.

During all that time we were near several harbours, such as Doublin, Waterfort, Corck and others but all without success. Saturday and this day we had good weather by which means we got into harbour.

Your most aff'te brother,
James Murray.

From November until April seems a long voyage from Scotland to America even in those days of primitive navigation, but another

---

* Atholl Records, p 433, Vol. III.

of the three additional companies was blown into Antigua and did
not arrive at New York until June.

With the activities of the preparations for the Ticonderoga
campaign a number of dispatches were sent to the Home Government and it is possible to follow more closely the fortunes of the
Black Watch.

The addition of these three companies raised the Regiment to
1,300 men, and we find among the official documents a petition from
Capt. Gordon Graham, endorsed by Lt. Col. Grant and General
Abercrombie, asking to be made Major in addition to Major Duncan Campbell, as follows:[*]

To His Excellency James Abercromby. Esq., General and Commander in Chief of all His Majesty's forces in North America,
etc., etc., etc.

The Memorial of Gordon Graham, eldest Captain in His
Majesty's 42nd Regiment of Foot in North America.

Humbly sheweth

That your memorialist hath had the honour to serve His
Majesty upwards of twenty-five years, twelve of which as Captain
in the above Regiment and is now eldest in that Rank.

That he hath served in Flanders and elsewhere during all the
last war, some part of which he was employed as Major of Brigade,
and had a commission as such from General St. Clair, on the
expedition under his command in the year 1746.

May it therefore please your Excellency to lay his case before
His Majesty that he in his great wisdom may be graciously pleased
to promote him to the Rank of Major when an opportunity offers,
all which is humbly submitted.

To His Excellency, James Abercromby, Esqr., General and
Commander in Chief of all his Majesty's forces in North America,
etc., etc., etc.

The Memorial of Colonel Francis Grant, Commanding his
Majesty's 42nd Regiment of Foot.

Humbly sheweth

That his Majesty having thought proper to augment the said
Regiment to 1,300 men by adding three additional companies to
it, and such a body of men being too numerous to be exercised and
disciplined by one Major only, your memoralist humbly conceives,
that it would be for the good of his Majesty's service to have
another Major added, as has been already done to the other two
Highland Battalions commanded by the Colonels Montgomery and
Fraser.

* Public Record Office W. O. 1.-1.

May it therefore please your Excellency to lay this matter before His Majesty that he in his great wisdom may be graciously pleased to give such directions thereupon as shall be thought necessary, all which is humbly submitted.

Colo. Grant, commanding His Majesty's 42nd Regiment, and Mr. Gordon Graham, a Captain in the same, having each of them presented me with a memorial, the contents of which I know to be true, I herewith transmit them to your Lordship, to be laid before the King, and to know His Royal Pleasure therein.

Extract from a letter signed James Abercromby to the Right Hon. Lord Viscount Barrington, dated New York, Apr. 28, 1758.

As will be seen later Capt. Graham became Major before hearing from the King.

The next dispatch which is of interest and which makes changes in the list of Commissioned Officers is as follows: Extract from letter signed by James Abercromby to the Right Honorable the Lord Viscount Barrington, dated Albany, May 27, 1758.[1]

In the list of the Commissions which I had the honour to transmit to your Lordship, by my last letter, you will have observed two vacancies in the 42nd Regiment, occasioned by the removal of Sir James Cockburn into the 48th which could not be filled up at the time my letter went away, as the gentlemen, whom it was proposed should purchase those vacancies were then at Albany,[2] and their answer not arrived; since that the Lieutenancy has been made out in the name of Mr. Patrick Balnevas, and bears date the 1st of April; and Mr. Elbert Hering succeeds to the Ensigncy, dated the 3rd of the same month."

Then we have the dispatch just before the battle from Abercrombie to Pitt, dated Camp at Lake George, June 29, 1758, saying: "Arrived Fort Edward on the 9th, where Lord Howe was encamped with the 42nd, 44th, and 55th Regiments and 4 companies of Rangers. Remainder of Regulars were at posts below on Hudson River and were working up the stores, etc. On the 17th Lord Howe marched to the Brook, half way between Fort Edward and the Lake with the 42nd, 44th, and 55th. This Half-way Brook was judged a proper post for the first Deposit in a Portage of 15 miles.[3] After the carriages had made several trips Lord Howe advanced to the Lake with the 42nd, 44th, and 55th."

---

1 Public record office W:O:L.-I.
2 His last letter had been written from New York, April 28th. If this were an earlier date it might indicate the winter quarters, but at this time the army was assembling at Albany for the seasons campaign. It will be noted as illustration that the Highlanders quartered at Stamford left there March 30.
3 For further information in regard to Halfway Brook, which is just north of the city of Glens Falls, see the "Halfway Brook in History," by James A. Holden in Vol. VI. of N. Y. State Hist. Assn. proceedings.

Attached to this letter is a report of troops at Lake George, June 29, 1758, and the roll of the 42nd was as follows:

"10 companies, 1 Lt. Colonel, 1 Major, 8 Captains, 18 Lieutenants, 7 Ensigns, 1 Chaplain, 1 Adjutant, 1 QuarterMaster, 1 Surgeon, 2 Mates, 40 Sergeants, 18 Drummers; Rank and File—981 fit for duty, 11 sick present, 6 in general hospital, 2 on command, 1,000 total. 1 drummer and 40 rank and file wanting to complete."

We find the solution of why there were only 1,000 of the Black Watch with the Ticonderoga expedition when its strength was known to be 1,300 at that time, in another extract of the Report of June 29th from Abercrombie to Pitt: "I have left two additional Companies of Lord John Murray's to garrison Fort Edward. The other additional company of the 42nd which was blown into Antego (Antigua), I hear is arrived at New York, which I have ordered up to Albany."

This is confirmed in more detail in a letter from Sir Robert Menzies to Mr. Murray of Strowan, dated Rannock, 6th Sept., 1758, in which is an extract from a letter received by Menzies from "Jamie Stewart."[*]

"That, after the additional Companies arrived in Fort Edward, the best men were picked out to compleat the Regiment in place of the sick and old men that were put in their place. That, as Capt. Reid was left behind sick at Albany, Capt. Murray was appointed to his company and Reid to the additionals, as Capt. Abercrombie was to Capt. Murray's Company. That the additional companies, with Captains Sterling, Reid, and Abercrombie, etc., were left at Fort Edward, where they had nothing to do but to garrison the Fort and divert themselves."

Everything is now in readiness for the attack on Ticonderogt and an army of six thousand three hundred seventy-seven regulars and nine thousand thirty-four provincials (Abercrombie to Pitt July 12, 1758) embarked at Lake George early on the morning of July 5th. There were nine hundred batteaux, a hundred and thirty-five whale boats and a large number of heavy flatboats carrying the artillery and from front to rear the line was six miles long.

---

[*] Atholl Records page, 444 Vo. III.

The Embarkation of Abercrombie's Army at Lake George, July 5, 1758

Parkman in his "Montcalm and Wolfe" paints the scene as follows: "The spectacle was superb; the brightness of the summer day; the romantic beauty of the scenery; the sheen and sparkle of those crystal waters; the countless islets, tufted with pine, birch, and fir; the bordering mountains, with their green summits and sunny crags; the flash of oars and glitter of weapons; the banners, the varied uniforms, and the notes of bugle, trumpet, bag-pipe, and drum, answered and prolonged by a hundred woodland echoes. 'I never beheld so delightful a prospect,' wrote a wounded officer at Albany a fortnight after.

"Rogers with the Rangers, and Gage with the light infantry, led the way in whaleboats, followed by Bradstreet with his corps of boatman, armed and drilled as soldiers. Then came the main body. The central column of regulars was commanded by Lord Howe, his own regiment, the fifty-fifth, in the van, followed by the Royal Americans, the twenty-seventh, forty-fourth, forty-sixth, and eightieth infantry, and the Highlanders of the forty-second, with their major, Duncan Campbell of Inverawe, silent and gloomy amid the general cheer, for his soul was dark with foreshadowings of death. With this central column came what are described as two floating castles, which were no doubt batteries to cover the landing of the troops. On the right hand and the left were the provincials, uniformed in blue, regiment after regiment, from Massachusetts, Connecticut, New York, New Jersey, and Rhode Island. Behind them all came the batteaux, loaded with stores and baggage, and the heavy flatboats that carried the artillery, while a rear-guard of provincials and regulars closed the long procession."

It will be unnecessary to go into the details of this disastrous campaign as it is not only well known to most of you but three papers bearing on the subject will be read at this meeting.* Briefly the army landed at the foot of Lake George the morning of the 6th and the afternoon of the same day Lord Howe at the head of a Ticonderoga party was killed at the outlet of Trout Brook. This is the beginning of the end as Lord Howe was the real head of the army. Abercrombie took until the eighth to make up his mind what to do and this interim gave the French time to build the fatal breastworks across the ridge about one-half mile west of the Fort and enabled Levis to arrive with reinforcements.

---

* Abercromby's full report to Pitt, under date of July 12, 1758, will be found in Mr. Holden's article on Lord Howe.

As the breastworks play a most important part in the Battle it will perhaps be well to again quote from Parkman who gives a most comprehensive description. "The trees that covered the ground were hewn down by thousands, the tops lopped off, and the trunks piled one upon another to form a massive breastwork. The line followed the top of the ridge, along which it zigzagged in such a manner that the whole front could be swept by flank-fires of musketry and grape. It was so high that nothing could be seen over it but the crowns of the soldiers' hats. The upper tier was formed of single logs, in which notches were cut to serve as loopholes; and in some places sods and bags of sand were piled along the top, with narrow spaces to fire through. From the central part of the line the ground sloped away like a natural glacis; while at the sides, and especially on the left, it was undulating and broken. Over this whole space, to the distance of a musket-shot from the works, the forest was cut down, and the trees left lying where they fell among the stumps, with tops turned outwards, forming one vast abattis, which, as a Massachusetts officer says, looked like a forest laid flat by a hurricane. But the most formidable obstruction was immediately along the front of the breastworks, where the ground was covered with heavy boughs, overlapping and interlaced, with sharpened points bristling into the face of the assailant like the quills of a porcupine. As these works were all of wood, no vestige of them remains. The earthworks now shown to tourists as the lines of Montcalm were begun four days after the battle to replace the log breastwork; and though on the same ground are not on the same plan."

Behind these breastworks the battalions of LaSarre and Languedoc were posted on the left under Bourlamaque, the first battalion of Berry with that of Royal Roussillon in the center under Montcalm and those of LaReine, Béarn and Guienne on the right under Lévis. A detachment of volunteers occupied the low grounds between the breastworks and the outlet of Lake George and on the side toward Lake Champlain were stationed 450 regulars and Canadians, about 3,600 in all.

It is always easy to criticise an event after it has occurred, but the result certainly shows that Abercrombie could not have planned his campaign more to the advantage of the French. He first gave them time to build those formidable breastworks and then instead of choosing any one of half a dozen plans which would have brought victory, he decided to throw his army unsupported by artillery, which was still at Lake George, at the strongest part of

the French position, he himself staying in safety at the saw mill
(about which we heard this afternoon in the able paper read by
Mr. Delano at the unveiling of the tablet) a mile and a half in
the rear of his army.*

The sad result is too well known to dwell on and we pass at
once to the part played by the Black Watch. They, with the 55th
were to have formed the reserve but impatient at being left in the
rear the Highlanders could not be restrained and were soon in the
front endeavoring to cut their way through the fallen trees with
their broadswords. Captain John Campbell, who was one of the
two soldiers presented to George II in 1743, with a few men, were
the only ones to force their way over the breastworks and they
were instantly dispatched with the bayonet.

Lieut. William Grant of the Regiment writes as follows:

"The attack began a little past one in the afternoon and about
two the fire became general on both sides. It was exceedingly heavy
and without intercession insomuch as the oldest soldier never saw
so furious and incessant a fire. The fire at Fontenoy was nothing
to it. I saw both."

An officer of the 55th regiment, of which Lord Howe had been
the commander, wrote as follows:

"With a mixture of esteem, grief and envy, I am penetrated
by the great loss and immortal glory acquired by the Highlanders
engaged in the late bloody affair. Impatient for the fray, they
rushed forward to the entrenchments which many of them actually
mounted, their intrepidity was rather animated than dampened by
witnessing their comrades fall on every side. They seemed more
anxious to avenge the fate of their deceased friends than to avoid
a like death. In their co-operation we trust soon to give a good
account of the enemy and of ourselves. There is much harmony
and friendship between the two regiments."

Even the French were impressed with the valor of the Black
Watch as Garneau writes in L'Histoire du Canada.'

"The Highlanders above all, under Lord John Murray, covered
themselves with glory. They formed the head of the troops con-

---

* This General James Abercrombie must not be confused with Sir Ralph
Abercrombie who led the Black Watch to victory in Egypt in 1801.
1 Translation by Bell, Page 539, Vol. I.

fronting the Canadians, their light and picturesque costume distinguishing them from all other soldiers amid the flame and smoke. This corps lost half of its men and 25 of its officers were killed or severely wounded."

Lossing writes, "The whole army seemed envious to excell but the Scotch Highland Regiment of Lord John Murray was foremost in the conflict and suffered the severest loss."[1]

The following letters from Captain Allan Campbell are of interest:

Camp at Lake George, 11th July, 1758.

Dr. Broyr.,—The 8th of this month we had a hot brush at the lines of Ticonderoga where we lost a considerable number of men and officers. The officers of your acquentance wounded are Major Campbell and his son. Both in their arms, and I hope will do well. Captain Stratchur slightly in the breast, Ltt. Archd. Campbell Sheriff Badly in the Breast, Lt. John Campbell Glendaruel slightly in the arm, Capt. Ltt. John Campbell Duneaves killed, Ltt. Hugh Macpherson ditto, Capt. Graham, Duchra, and Broyr. Both wounded slightly and several other offrs. of the Regt. but not of your acquentance are killed and wounded.

Our Regt. acquired great glory by their good hehaviour of both men and officers, tho' we were unsuccessfull. I have the pleasure to aquent you that both my nephew George and I eskeaped without a scratch, tho' both in the heat of the action. George is a pritty Lad: he's now a Ltt. in Coll. Gages Regt. of Lt. Infantry. Your son the Major was well about 2 months ago at Philadelphia. We are now at the end of Lake George Encampt. I have told you now all the news that can occurr to me or that I have time to write you, and I thought it my duty to acquent you and my other Broyrs. of my being well after a smart action. I have no time to write you more being excessively hurried having no Body to assist me in the affairs of my Company having my three Ltts. killed or wounded viz. Ltt. Balie killed and Ltts. Archd. Campbell and William Grant wounded. I'll write you very fully in my nixt. My best wishes to my sister, to your family and all our friends, and I am Dr. Bryr, your most affec. and Lov. Broyr, while

Allan Campbell.

New York, 6th January 1759.

Dr. Brother,—I writt you the 11th July in a great hurry after our retreat from Ticonderoga to let you know of mine and George's welfair, after that unlucky afair, where severall of our friends and a great many worthy Fellows suffer'd. Our Regt. lost more than any other Corps at the attack of the Lines. We have had killed

1 Lossing's Pictorial Field Book of the Revolution. Page 119, Vol. 1.

and wounded since the beginning of the Campaign 520 (officers included) of which about 300 were left dead on the field or have dyed of their wounds, and of 37 officers that were present with the Regt. that day 11 only came off unhurt, of which number I was lucky enough to be one.

You would certainly hear before now of poor Major Campbell Inveraw's death, he liv'd about a fortnight after he receiv'd his wound, the Doctors thought it necessary that his arm should be cut off, and he dyed soon after the operation at Fort Edward, all the rest of our wounded officers are quite recover'd except his son, Sandy, Jock Campbell Glendaruel, and Archie Shirreff, but they are out of all danger, only their cure will be tedious.

Poor George had a narrow escape the day we landed at the French end of the Lake, having had a scratch along the face with a musquet Ball. He was in a smart little action that happen'd in the woods a mounth afterwards between a detachment of 500 of our army under the command of Major Rogers and much the same number of Indians French and Canadians, where the latter were repulsed with the loss of 100 men, and I assure you his behaviour at that affair was much aplauded by his Broyr. officers on their return to the Army.

He's now second oldest Lieut. in General Gage's Regt. of light arm'd infantry, for which he's obliged to the late Major Campbell, Inveraw; and as they talk at present of agmenting that corps, he'll have a good chance of getting Higher up, and in any event he's better off by being so High in that Regt. as they are now an Establish'd Corps, than if he had staid in ours, where he could be but a young Lieut. His Coll. has a great regard for him, and very Deservedly for he's a lad of good morals, a good spirit ,and very fit for his Business. He has acted as Adjutant to that Regt. since July last, by which he has nothing yet but Troble, there being no Adjutant allow'd, and that his Collonel means it for him; if he's lucky enough to get that, I think he's very well provided for for the time he has served.

I have advanc'd him Twenty Guineas for which he gave me a Bill on you. I hope you'll not Disaprove of my conduct for doing it, nor blame him for running so much short, when I explain to you the cause of it; its trew he came over very well Riged out, but his changing Corps put him under a necessity of Buying new Regimentals, as these Differ in Colours from the rest of the Army, being Brown, besides his expense must be greater upon his first comming in among Strangers, and he had the misfortune of being sent a recruiting last winter, which really is a misfortune to an officer in this Country unless he is very carfull and happens to be successful, and I belive George lost by it. This I ashure you is truth, and when you consider it was owing to these accidents, that he could not possibly guard against, I am hopfull you'l easily forgive him. I was likewise oblig'd to advance our Unkle Corries' son, Colin,, Twenty two Pounds eighteen shillings and tenpence or he must have gone naked, having lost all his things at Fort William Henry. I have sent both Bills to Brother Robert. George and Colin are sent this winter a Recruiting to Pensilvania.

I had a letter dated the 30 Novr. from my nephew, the Major, from where Fort du Quesne stood, he was then very well. I expect dayly to hear from him, he's had as troublesome and Fatigueing Campaign of it, as ever any Body had, our Army has been above a Month in Winter Quarters befor thers got to Fort du Quesne, which the French burnt upon ther near aproach, and an immense long march they have to get back to Philadelphia, wher ther Regt. is to be Quarter's this winter, and where I intend to go and see him, when I hear of ther arrival, its about 100 miles from this place that our Regt. is now quartere'd in.

We long much for a Pacquet here having no news from Europe for some months, I take the opportunity of writing you now by the Kennington Man of War that carries home General Abercrombie. * * * * *

There is no News here at Present. All our Friends in this Country are Well. Remember my best wishes to my Sister, and the rest of your Family whom may God Almighty bless and I ever am, Dr. Brother, your affec. and Lov. Broyr.

Allan Campbell.

FOOT NOTE—Some of the names in the two preceding letters from Capt. Campbell are interesting because they illustrate the Scottish custom of using name of estate rather than the family or given name. This was often necessary to distinguish between several of same name. Captain Stratchur is Captain John Campbell of Stratchur, there are also John Campbells of Duneavis, and of Glendaruel. Archie Sherreff is Lieut. Archibald Campbell, son of the Sheriff of Argyle. Duchra is Capt. Thomas Graeme of Duchray. George and "the Major" are sons of John Campbell of Barcaldine—George Campbell was appointed Ensign in the 42d in 1756, promoted Lieut. in Gage's Regiment 1757, and killed at Havana 1762. "The Major" was Alexander Campbell, Major in the 77th (Montgomery Highlanders). Unkle Corries is John Campbell of Corries and his son Colin was evidently at the massacre at Fort William Henry in August 1757. Fort du Quesne was the French fort at what is now Pittsburgh.

I also give in full the letter written by Capt. James Murray to his brother, Mr. Murray of Strowan, dated Albany, July 19, 1758, as his description of the country and the events during and after the battle lend color to the picture.[1]

---

1 Atholl Records. Page 438, Vol. 3.

"My Dear Brother:—The last letter I wrote you was dated
from Fort Edward camp about 18th June. We proceeded on to
Lake George where Fort William Henry formerly stood which was
taken and destroyed by the French last year, where we remained
until the 5th curt. and then the whole army embarked on the lake
in batteaux that hold 23 men with a month's provisions all the
artillery stores was likewise embarked, and everything else belonging to an army. We were divided into brigades. There was in all
about 5,000 regulars and 12,000 provincials. We had also light
infantry and rangers who had whale-boats which are the lightest
and best going boats that can be made. We put off about 8 and got
fairly into the lake which I took to be about 20 miles long and not
above two miles at the broadest part of it. There are several small
islands which are quite covered with wood and all around the lake
is very hilly and quite covered with woods, as the most part of the
country is, at least what I have seen on't.

This lake abounds in fine trout the meat of which is red,
pearch, suckers and several other sorts of fish. There is also plenty
of beavers. On the side of the lake there is plenty of deer but I
have not seen any since I came to the country. Sometimes when
I have been out on command I have killed rattle snakes about four
feet long and as thick as the small of one's leg, with 18 rattles,
which altogether might be about four inches long. They say some
have twenty or more. They have both teeth and a sting. The
rattles being at the tail makes them that they can stand up on end
and spring a short way at one. When touched they make a great
noise with their rattles. Their bite is not so bad as called for it
can be easily cured with oil or salt. They smell exactly like a
goat, rather ranker if possible before they are seized but afterwards
have almost no smell at all. They make the richest and best soup
that can be which I eat of and like much. The meat is but insipid.

The 6th we disembarked at the lower end of the lake. In the
morning out light infantry and rangers had some skirmishing with
the French pickets. Lord Howe was killed at the second shot and
he is very much regretted. There was taken that day about 150
prisoners, five of whom were officers. They had a great many killed
so that very few of their pickets escaped which consisted in all
of about 350.

The next day being the 7th, we were making preparations to
invest a fort called Theenderora which is five miles from Lake
George and is situate on a neck of land that runs into Lake Champlain. As to the dimensions of that lake I can't say, and marched

within a mile and half of it that evening. The next morning the light infantry made the French sentries and small posts retire to their entrenchments for the French had an encampment about half a cannon shot before their fort, and were entrenched after the following manner: They had large cut trees one laid above another a man's height and in the outside there was brush and logs for about 15 paces from it which made it impossible to force their breastworks without cannon which we had not taken up that length as then. They were also under cover of the fort or if we could beat them out of their trenches, they could have retired pretty safely.

Between one and two we marched up and attacked the trenches and got within twenty paces of them and had as hot a fire for about three hours as possibly could be, we all the time seeing but their hats and the end of their muskets. About half an hour before we were obliged to retire I received a shot through my thigh after which I stayed a few minutes but finding if I stayed any longer my thigh would turn stiff and losing a great deal of blood I with help got into the road and that evening with Capt. Gordon Graham, our paymaster, got into a whaleboat and against the next morning got to the upper end of Lake George and was transported down here. I am confined to my bed but the surgeons say my wound looks as well as can be expected, nor is there any sort of danger in it as it has only grazed the bone, so I shall be well soon again. I am in perfect good health, have a good appetite and sleep tolerably well.

Our regiment has suffered much. There was the captain, lieutenant and six subalterns killed on the spot and since the major and the lieutenant have died of their wounds. The colonel, four captains, and twelve subalterns are wounded. 180 men killed and 280 wounded. None of the other regiments' losses were near so great. Capt. Stewart was not touched, Capt. Sterling nor Farquharson were not there so are well, but Lieut. Farquharson's younger brother was killed. Lieut. David Mills, my lieutenant, is not ill wounded and is pretty well, so if you would inform his father-in-law, Mr. Hamilton, of Hutcheson, who stays near Glasgow, you would oblige me. Neil Stewart at Perth knows him.

I received a letter from Lord John 15th May letting me know you are all well which gave me a great deal of pleasure but it would much more so to hear from some of you for it is very long since I had that satisfaction, the last being at Ireland, for Lord John wrote me no particulars.

Offer my humble duty to my dear mother and elsewhere due and best love to dear Lady Charlotte, Lady Sinclair, George, Charlotte and Invercauld, and my best blessing attend all the young ones. My kind compliments to Shusy Moray and tell her I had her hair about my neck when I received my wound which might have probably gone to my heart if it had not been wounded already.

I am ever your most effectionate brother,

James Murray.

Thus had the army which landed so proudly two days before been disastrously repulsed, with a loss in killed and wounded and missing of nineteen hundred and forty-four officers and men. In his report of July 12, 1758, Abercrombie gives the casualty of the 42nd as follows:

"Killed—Capt. Lt. John Campbell; Lts. George Farquharson, Hugh McPherson, |William Bailey, |John Sutherland; Ensigns Peter Stewart and George Rattray.

Wounded—Major Duncan Campbell; Captains Gordon Graham, Thomas Graeme, John Campbell, James Stewart, James Murray; Lieutenants William -Grant, Robert Gray, John Campbell, James Grant, John Graham, Alexander Campbell, Alexander McIntosh, Archibald Campbell, David Mill,* Patrick Balnevis; Ensigns John Smith and Peter Grant.

Summary—1 major wounded, captains 1 killed, 4 wounded; lieutenants 4 killed, 11 wounded; ensigns 2 killed, 2 wounded; adjutants 1 wounded; quarter master 1 wounded; sergeants 6 killed, 13 wounded, rank and file 190 killed, 265 wounded."

Stewart of Garth writes as follows:

"Of these the 42nd regiment had 8 officers, 9 serjeants, and 297 men killed, and 17 officers, 10 serjeants, and 306 soldiers wounded. The officers were, Major Duncan Campbell of Inverawe, Captain John Campbell, Lieutenants George Farquharson, Hugh McPherson, William Baillie, and John Sutherland; Ensigns Patrick Stewart of Bonskied and George Rattray killed; Captains Gordon Graham, Thomas Graham of Duchray, John Campbell of Strachur, James Stewart of Urrad, James Murray (afterward General); Lieutenants James Grant, Robert Gray, John Campbell, William Grant, John Graham, brother of Duchray, Alexander Campbell, Alexander Mackintosh, Archibald Campbell, David Miller, Patrick Balneaves; and Ensigns John Smith and Peter Grant, wounded."

---

* This name is given in various places as MILL, MILLS, MILLER and MILNE. The Duke of Atholl is authority for the statement that MILNE is correct.

Capt. James Murray writes from Albany 17th August, 1758:[1] "As I observed in my last, our regiment has suffered greatly. The Major has since died of his wounds, Sandy Farquharson has got his lieutenancy by seniority which one would not have thought that the youngest ensign of the additionals would have been so soon a lieutenant. I am recovering pretty well and can walk about although I am much pained in my knee but hope will be able to soon joint the regiment.

Capt. James Stewart writes 14th July from Lake George:[2] "That all the Captains were wounded, less or more, excepting Captains McNeil and Allan Campbell, that Major Campbell got his right arm wounded, but not dangerous and his son, Lieutenant Alexander Campbell had his arm broke betwixt the elbow and shoulder, but he was in a good way."

Parkman states that Lt. Alexander Campbell was severely wounded but reached Scotland alive and died in Glasgow.[3]

Abercrombie reports to Pitt from Lake George, Aug. 19, 1758; "Major Duncan Campbell of the 42nd who was wounded in the arm at the battle on the 8th was obliged to have it cut off and died soon thereafter."

It would seem therefore that the wounds of Major Campbell and his son were not necessarily fatal and that modern surgery would have cured them. The following however, taken from Garneau's L'Histoire du Canada might explain the unexpected mortality. "Scarcely any of the wounded Highlanders ever recovered and even those sent home as invalids; their sores cankered, owing to the broken glass, ragged bits of metal, etc., used by the Canadians instead of shot."[5]

Or this extract from letter of Brig. General James Wolfe to Lord George Sackville:

Halifax 24" May 1758.
"Some of the Regiments of this Army have 300 or 400 men eat up with the Scurvey. All of them that are wounded or hurt by any accident run great risks of their lives from the corrupted state of the blood."

1. Atholl Records, p. 444, Vol. III.
2. Atholl Records, p. 443, Vol. III.
3. Montcalm and Wolfe, p. 435, Vol. II.
4. Public Record Office, C.O.5. 50.
5. Translation by Bell, page 539, Vol. I.

Original headstone at Grave of Major Duncan Campbell of Inverawe.
(Jane McCrea lot in Union Cemetery, between Fort Edward and Hudson Falls

"The curious part of the barbarity is that the scoundrels of Contractors can afford the fresh meat in many places and circumstances as cheap as the salt."

Abercrombie states in his report of July 12, 1758, "I sent the wounded officers and the men that could be moved to Fort Edward and Albany."

Major Campbell was sent to Fort Edward and upon his death nine days after the battle he was buried in the family lot of the Gilchrists, in the old cemetery at Fort Edward. The body was moved to the Gilchrist lot in the new Union cemetery between Sandy Hill and Fort Edward in 1871, and in 1920 was moved again to the Jane McCrea lot in the same cemetery. The original stone may still be seen and bears the inscription: "Here Lyes the body of Duncan Campbell of Inversaw, Esqr Major to The old Highland Regt. Aged 55 Years. Who died The 17th July, 1758, of wounds he received in the attack of the retrenchments of Ticonderoga or Carillon, 8th July, 1758."

Stewart of Garth says, "The old Highland Regiment having suffered so severely * * * * they were not employed again that year."

In the N. Y. Colonial Records, however, we find that some regulars of the 42nd and 6th Regts. amounting to 155 men (probably one company of each) were with Bradstreet in his exposition against Fort Frontenac.[1]

In Abercrombie's report of Aug. 19, 1758, he states that part of the additional companies of the 42nd were sent to reinforce Brig. General Provost at Fort Edward and that one company of the 42nd and some of the recovering men were stationed at Albany. From this it might be inferred that the only part of the Black Watch fit for duty were the three additional companies which had not been in the battle of July 8th and it is possible that the one company of the 42nd that had been blown out of its course to Antigua and had not arrived at New York until June did not get further north than Albany. The winter quarters of the 42nd for 1758 were at New York. (Abercrombie to Pitt, No. 25, 1758.)[2]

The official title is now changed to the "42nd or Royal Regi-

---

1. N. Y. Col. manuscript O'Callaghan's, p. 827, Vol. 10.
2. Public Record Office C. O. 5: 50.

ment of foot," and the regiment is commonly called the Royal
Highlanders. It has erroneously been stated that the Black Watch
was granted this honor of being a "Royal" regiment because of its
gallantry at Ticonderoga, but it is all the more to its credit that it
had earned this distinction before the battle at Ticonderoga. The
title was granted by special warrant dated July 22, 1758, while the
news of the defeat did not reach London until the arrival of
Abercrombie's aid de camp with dispatches Aug. 20, 1758.

A copy of the warrant is as follows:
George R

We being desirous to distinguish Our Forty Second Regiment
of Foot with some mark of Our Royal favor, Our Will and Pleasure therefore is, and we do hereby direct, that from henceforth
Our said regiment be called, and distinguished by the title and
name of Our Forty-Second, or Royal Highland Regiment of Foot,
in all commissions, orders, and writings, that shall hereafter be
made out, or issued for and concerning the said regiment. Given
at Our Court at Kensington this 22nd day of July 1758, in the
thirty second year of Our reign. By His Majesty's command.
                         (Signed)   BARRINGTON.

The vacancies occasioned in the 42nd were filled up in regular
succession and the seven companies which had been ordered at the
same time as the change of title were immediately recruited. These
were completed in three months and embodied at Perth, October
1758, each company being 120 men strong, all with few exceptions
Highlanders and hardy and temperate in their habits. (Lord John
Murray's orders were preemptory that none but Highlanders be
taken, but a few O'Donnels, O'Lachlans and O'Briens passed muster
as Mac Donnels, MacLachlans and Mac Briars.)

These seven companies with the three additional companies
raised in 1757 were formed into a Second Battalion. The officers
appointed to the seven new companies were Robert Anstruther,
who was senior captain and served as Major, Francis MacLean,
Alexander Sinclair, John Stewart of Stenton, William Murray of
Lintrose, Archibald Campbell, Alexander Reid, and Robert Arbuthnot, to be captains; Alexander MacLean, George Grant, George
Sinclair, Gordon Clunes, Adam Stewart, John Robertson, son of
Lude, John Grant, James Fraser, George Leslie, John Campbell,

Alexander Stewart, Duncan Richardson and Robert Robertson, to be lieutenants and Patrick Sinclair, John MacIntosh, James MacDuff, Thomas Fletcher, Alexander Donaldson, William MacLean, and William Brown, to be ensigns.

The seven new companies embarked for the West Indies where they joined with the Old Bluffs, Kings, 6th, 63rd, 64th, 800 marines and a detachment of artillery amounting in all to 5,560 men under the command of Major Generals Hopson and Barrington and of Brigadier Generals Haldane, Armiger, Trapaud and Clavering, in an exposition against Martinique and Gaudaloupe. This resulted in the capture of Gaudaloupe but was not altogether a success and a great many men were lost by fever and sickness. Of the Royal Highlanders Ensign MacLean was killed, Lieutenants MacLean, Leslie, Sinclair and Robertson were wounded, and Major Anstruther and Captain Arbuthnot died of the fever. One hundred and six privates were killed, wounded or died of disease.

This was a severe initiation for the new recruits who had been herding sheep on their native hills nine months before, but as has always been the case with the Black Watch they acquitted themselves with distinction. The seven companies were then embarked for New York to join the First Battalion where they arrived in July. They just missed being at the capture of Ticonderoga. Major Gordon Graham was ordered at the end of July by General Amherst then at Crown Point to take command of the seven companies and to march them up to Oswego. In August they were ordered to join the First Battalion, Capt. Stewart with 150 men being left at Oswego and the First and Second Battalions, now united, served together for the rest of the campaign.

We will now return to the Veterans of the previous year. After wintering in New York (or on Long Island, as another authority states) the old Black Watch now the first Battalion of the Royal Highlanders, recruited again to its full strength and the three additional companies now a part of the Second Battalion, joined Amherst at Fort Edward in June, 1759.* Col. Grant of the 42nd with the Royal Highlanders and light infantry of the army

* See Appendix for extracts from Commissary Wilsons Orderly Book for record of daily service of Black Watch in Ticonderoga and Crown Point campaign.

moved forward to Lake George the 20th and the main part of the army followed on the 21st. For five years now Lake George had been the annual mustering place of armies.

The campaign this season comprehended three very important enterprises—Wolfe was to attack Quebec from Lower Canada, Prideaux was to proceed against Niagara, and Amherst, now Commander in Chief and successor of General Abercrombie, was to drive the French from Lake Champlain and if possible join Wolfe on the St. Lawrence.

The army under Amherst consisted of the Royals, 17th, 27th, Royal Highlanders, two battalions of the 55th, Montgomery's Highlanders, nine battalions of Provincials, and a battalion of light infantry and a body of Rangers and Indians with a detachment of artillery. When joined by the 2d battalion of the Royal Americans from the West Indies, this army amounted to 14,500 men.

Major Alexander Campbell of the 77th writes from Fort Edward, June 19th, 1759:

"Our General is beloved by his soldiers, Honoured and Esteem'd by his officers, Carful of mens lives and healths, in short he is the man I would choose to serve under of any I know in the service. Our Regiment are healthy and in High spirits as are the whole army, and I hope we soon will stricke a stroke that will bring credite and Glory to our General and Army and Satisfaction to our Country and friends."

Amherst never remained long in one place without building a fort. Fortified places were built at intervals of three or four miles along the road to Fort Edward and especially at the station called Halfway Brook, while for the whole distance a broad belt of wood on both sides was cut down and burned to deprive a skulking enemy of cover. At Lake George he started a fort, now called Fort George, the ruins of which are in the Lake George Battle Ground Park of which this Association is custodian.

July 21st, 1759, Lake George again witnessed a military pageant as the army embarked for its second attack on Fort Ticonderoga. At daylight they landed, beat back a French detachment

and marched by the portage road to the sawmill. There was little
resistance and the army marched to the former line of entrenchments which had proved so fatal to Abercrombie. These had been
reconstructed partly of earth and partly of logs, and as the French
made no attempt at their defence the English encamped along their
front and found them excellent shelter from the cannon of the fort.
It is the general impression that the French retreated with only
faint resistance and that there was hardly a shot fired at the
second attempt to capture Fort Carrillon but the following letter
from Capt. Murray would correct this impression:

"Camp at the Lines of Burning Theanderoga, 27 July, 1758.

My Dear Brother:—I write you these few lines to acquaint you
that I am in perfect good health and that the army landed at this
end of the lake the 22nd, invested the Fort the 23rd and was very
buisy carying on the worcks till the 26th in the night, at which time
we had three batteries ready to open, when the enemy abbandoned
and set fire to the fort. During the time that the enemy remained
they could not keep a hotter fire, for I dare say that fired ten
thousand cannon shott and five hundred bombs and I don't believe
there has been forty men killed and wounded during that hott fire,
altho' all the Bombs fell in different parts among us and that we
were nigh point blank of the cannon shott but the line that had
been of so much hurt to us last year saved our men this.
                    Your most afft. Brother, James Murray."

I also add Amherst's report to Governor James DeLancey:

                    Camp at Ticonderoga 27th July 1759.

Sir:—
On Saturday morning last I embarked with the army at Lake
George, the next day landed without opposition and proceeded to
the saw mills, and took post on the commanding grounds, meeting
only a trifling opposition from the enemy. We lay on our arms all
night and early on the 23rd we continued our march to the ground
which I took possession of in the forenoon, the enemy having
abandoned the lines without destroying them, first having carried
off their effects as well as sent away the greatest part of their
troops. As soon as I was set down before the place and after having
reconnoitered it, I ordered the trenches to be opened and batteries
to be made, which were finished last night, and were to have opened
at break of day, but the enemy did not think proper to wait till
then, having about ten of the clock yesterday evening blown up a

part of the Fort, and made their escape all to about 20 deserters. Our loss considering the fire we sustained is inconsiderable. We have only two officers killed, vis. Colonel Townshend, Deputy Adjutant General and Ensign Harrison of late Forbe's.

Bourlamaque had on receipt of orders from Vandreuil retired down Lake Champlain leaving four hundred men under Hebecourt to defend the fort as long as possible and then to abandon Ticonderoga and later when pressed Crown Point and to retreat to Isle-oux-Noix at the outlet of Lake Champlain, where defense was to be made to the last extremity. When the English battery was ready to open fire Hebecourt saw that further resistance was useless and lighting a slow match to the magazine the French escaped down the lake in their boats and a few hours later an explosion which hurled one bastion of old Fort Carrillon skyward shook the promontory. Thus did French Carillon become English Ticonderoga and "Ticonderoga 1758-9" should be among the battle honors to be borne on the colors of the Black Watch. It is true that these honorary distinctions are awarded by the King only in case of victory but Ticonderoga 1758-9 would certainly be as much a victory as "South Africa 1899-1902," which has been granted. South Africa was not all victory and the Black Watch suffered at Magersfontein as it did at Ticonderoga under Abercrombie.

The length of time elapsed since the battle would also be no objection to the honor being now granted as it was not until 1910, two and one half centuries later that the armies that upheld British honor on the Coast of Morocco were authorized to bear "Tangier 1662-1680" on their colors and appointments.

Ticonderoga is the one place on the American continent where Great Britain and France, Canada and the United States can all unite on one common ground. The Yankees and British can meet here and clasp hands over the time when they once fought together and there is not even a sectional feeling which detracts from the unanimity. The North, South, East and West of the United States all join with equal fervor. Each nation had its defeats here at different times but each also had its victories. Therefore there is no battle honor which could be conferred on any British regiment that would please more people of different nations than "Ticon-

FORT EDWARD, 1759

deroga 1758-9." The fact that there is at present in the village of
Ticonderoga a public library and historical building dedicated to
a British Regiment, even though this same regiment in its line of
duty fought against us in a later war, is sufficient proof that we
consider Ticonderoga of international history and above matters
of local prejudice.

The rest of the story is soon told. Crown Point was captured
and the army was to have moved forward to Isle oux-Noix and to
the St. Lawrence but a succession of storms so delayed operations
that further active movements were abandoned for the remainder
of the season. Amherst profiting by the fatal precipitation of his
predecessor was slow but sure and in this campaign was successful
in every enterprise that he undertook.

After the capture of Crown Point the army under Amherst
was mainly employed in building operations on Lake Champlain,
Fort Amherst at Crown Point and Fort Ticonderoga in place of
old Fort Carrillon at Ticonderoga. The Black Watch was stationed
at Crown Point and helped to build Fort Amherst. In November,
they went into camp for the winter and in his report of "Garrisons
and Winter Quarters of His Majesty's forces in North America
under the command of His Excellency, Major General Amherst,
Headquarters at New York, 15 Dec., 1759" in the Public Record
Office, the stations of the Black Watch were as follows: 1st
Battalion Royal Highland Regiment, 1 company Halfway Brook,
5 companies Fort Edward, 1 company Fort Miller, 1 company
Saratoga, 1 company Stillwater and 1 company Halfmoon, 2d
Battalion Royal Highland Regiment, Albany, one Battalion of
the Inniskilling (27th Foot) and two companies of the Rangers
were left at Crown Point, six companies Late Brig. Gen'l Forbe's
(17th Foot) at Ticonderoga, and four companies 17th Foot at Fort
George. The following season (1760) the Black Watch was with
Amherst at the capture of Montreal which was the end of the
French domain on the American Continent.

In 1761 the Black Watch with ten regiments embarked for
Barbadoes there to join an armament against Martinique and
Havana. After the surrender of Havana, the first battalion of the
42nd and Montgomery's Highlanders embarked for New York

which they reached in the end of October, 1762. Before leaving Cuba most of the second battalion of the 42nd fit for service were consolidated with the first, and the remainder shipped to Scotland where they were reduced the following year.

The Black Watch was stationed at Albany until the summer of 1763, when they, with a detachment of Montgomery's Highlanders and another of the 60th, under command of Col. Henry Boquet were sent to the relief of Fort Pitt then besieged by the Indians. The 42nd passed the winter at Fort Pitt and during the summer of 1764, eight companies were sent with the army of Boquet against the Ohio Indians. After subduing the Indians they returned to Fort Pitt, January 1765. The regiment remained in Pennsylvania until the month of July, 1767, when it embarked at Philadalphia for Ireland. Such of the men who preferred to remain in America were permitted to join other regiments. These volunteers were so numerous that along with those who had been previously sent home disabled and others discharged and settled in America, the regiment that returned was very small in proportion to that which had left Scotland.

Let us now turn our attention to Major Duncan Campbell as not only would no sketch of the Black Watch of Ticonderoga be complete without the legend with which his name is associated, but we are perhaps more interested in him than any other officer of the Regiment of that time because he lies buried in the cemetry midway between Hudson Falls (formerly Sandy Hill) and Fort Edward. The other officers and men who were killed July 8, 1758, were doubtless buried on the field of battle and if the graves were ever marked, these marks have long since been destroyed.

No ghost story is more widely known or better authenticated than that of Duncan Campbell of Inverawe. It has been made the subject of an address before this Association by the late Robert O. Bascom at the meeting of July 30, 1901, and has been repeated in many forms and in various publications but it will bear still one more repetition. The following is taken from Parkman's "Montcalm and Wolfe" and is the story as was told by Dean Stanley and endorsed by the family of the hero of the tale:

AT INVERAWE

Old Inverawe House from the River Awe with Ben Cruachan in the background.

View from the West. X marks the window of the Ghost Room.

Bridge over the Awe built by Captain William Piman about 1756

"The ancient castle of Inverawe stands by the banks of the Awe, in the midst of the wild and picturesque scenery of the Western Highlands. Late one evening, before the middle of the last century, as the laird, Duncan Campbell, sat alone in the old hall, there was a loud knocking at the gate; and, opening it, he saw a stranger, with torn clothing and kilt besmeared with blood, who in a breathless voice begged for asylum. He went on to say that he had killed a man in a fray, and that the pursuers were at his heels. Campbell promised to shelter him. "Swear on your dirk!"* said the stranger; and Campbell swore. He then led him to a secret recess in the depths of the castle. Scarcely was he hidden when again there was a loud knocking at the gate, and two armed men appeared. "Your cousin Donald has been murdered, and we are looking for the murderer!" Campbell, remembering his oath, professed to have no knowledge of the fugitive; and the men went on their way. The laird, in great agitation, lay down to rest in a large dark room where at length he fell asleep. Waking suddenly in bewilderment and terror, he saw the ghost of the murdered Donald standing by his bedside, and heard a hollow voice pronounce the words: "Inverawe! Inverawe! blood has been shed. Shield not the murderer." In the morning Campbell went to the hiding place of the guilty man and told him that he could harbor him no longer. "You have sworn on your dirk" he replied; and the laird of Inverawe, greatly perplexed and troubled, made a compromise between conflicting duties, promised not to betray his guest, led him to the neighboring mountain (Ben Cruachan) and hid him in a cave.

In the next night, as he lay tossing in feverish slumbers, the same stern voice awoke him, the ghost of his cousin Donald stood again at his bedside, and again he heard the same appalling words: "Inverawe! Inverawe! blood has been shed. Shield not the murderer!" At break of day he hastened, in strange agitation, to the cave; but it was empty, the stranger had gone. At night, as he strove in vain to sleep, the vision appeared once more, ghastly pale,

---

* The oath of the Campbells of Inverawe was by Ben Cruachan.
Bibliography of the Legend of Duncan Campbell of Inverawe.
A. P. Stanley, "Inverawe and Ticonderoga," Fraser's Magazine, Oct. 1880.
Robert Louis Stevenson, poem on "Ticonderoga," Scribner's Magazine, December, 1887.
Francis Parkman, Appendix G. "Montcalm and Wolfe," and "Historical Handbook of the Northern Tour," Boston, 1885.
Robert O. Bascom, "New York State Historical Proceedings," Vol. II., "Fort Edward Book," pages 80–88.
C. F. Gordon Cumming in the Atlantic Monthly, September, 1884.
W. Max Reid, "Lake George and Lake Champlain".
Sir Thomas Dick Lauder, "Tales of the Highlands."
Winsor's Critical and Narrative History of the United States.
Lord Archibald Campbell, "Records of Argyle," William Blackwood & Sons, 1885.
"The Magazine of History," July, 1906.
"Book of Dreams and Ghosts," Longman's, 1897.

but less stern of aspect than before. "Farewell, Inverawe!" it said; "Farewell, till we meet at TICONDEROGA!"

The strange name dwelt in Campbell's memory. He had joined the Black Watch, or Forty-Second Regiment, then employed in keeping order in the turbulent Highlands. In time he became its major; and, a year or two after the war broke out, he went with it to America. Here, to his horror, he learned that it was ordered to the attack of Ticonderoga. His story was well known among his brother officers. They combined among themselves to disarm his fears; and when they reached the fatal spot they told him on the eve of the battle, "This is not Ticonderoga; we are not there yet; this is Fort George."[1] But in the morning he came to them with haggard looks. "I have seen him! You have deceived me! He came to my tent last night! This is Ticonderoga! I shall die today!" and his prediction was fulfilled."

As will be seen by the preceding pages, Inverawe lived nine days after the battle and was not even mortally wounded if it had been possible in those times to have had antiseptic treatment, but the real point of the legend is that he had been warned of Ticonderoga when he did not know there was such a place, years before there was any prospect of his being sent there and when Ticonderoga was only the Indian name for a point of land on a lake in the wilderness of a far off continent.

To one interested no place could be more fascinating than old Inverawe'[2] everything connected with it breathes of legend and romance and naturally this was one of the first places visited in our Black Watch pilgrimage last summer. Taynuilt, the railroad station nearest Inverawe is a small village across the Awe and about a mile away as the crow flies, but to drive to our destination, one must follow the road two miles up the River to the old bridge which was being built at the time that the Major left for the war in America in 1756. The builder was Captain William Pitman apparently a good friend of Duncan of Inverawe as he charged him with the safe keeping during his absence of his daughter Janet and his favorite dog. History does not record what happened to the dog but the Captain married the daughter and in time Inverawe became her property.

---

1. More probably Fort Carrillon.
2. Inver means "the mouth of," therefore the mouth of the River Awe.

Photo by Miss Dorothea E. Seaton, Edinburgh

A Corner of the Ghost Room

Two Views of Library

After crossing the Awe the road turns down the north side of the River and winds through a magnificent park, some of the trees of which must certainly have been there before the Major's time. This is all the more remarkable because with the exception of the parks of the private estates, Scotland is nearly a treeless country and even the mountains and wild land which with us would be covered with forests, have there only grass and heather. Then at the end of a delightful four mile drive was old Inverawe house and a most cordial and hospitable welcome from its present owner.

The old house has had many additions in the past one hundred and fifty years but the entrance hall and the main part of the building and particularly the room where Duncan Campbell saw the ghost, are still very much as they were in his time. We endeavored to learn as much as possible of the family history of the Campbells of Inverawe, but like the records of the Black Watch of that time, there was in 1910, little left but tradition.

The Campbells of Inverawe

Twenty years have passed since the account of the Black Watch at Ticonderoga as written for the 1910 meeting of the New York State Historical Association was published, and while we regret that very little can be added, we are pleased to say that few corrections have had to be made in the story as then told. It was thought that the records of the Regiment of the 18th Century were discovered in 1913 among the military manuscripts in the Royal United Service Institution, but while they purported to be the original records, careful examination disclosed that they had been written early in the nineteenth century so nothing new was learned of the Regiment of the Ticonderoga period. The preceding pages therefore are practically unchanged.

The part, however, about the family history of Major Duncan Campbell of Inverawe has been entirely rewritten. We are indebted for this additional information to the descendants of Alexander, a brother of Duncan of Inverawe, to the late Major Sir Duncan Campbell of Barcaldine, to the late Captain Douglas Wimberly, and others. No one feature of the Black Watch at Ticonderoga has been of such general interest as the ghost story of its Major, Duncan Campbell of Inverawe, and the straightening out of the family puzzle which was such a mystery in 1910 has been a fascinating study.

The Major's memory has been honored recently by two celebrations. In 1920 when his bones were moved to the Jane McCrea enclosure, just inside the main gate of the Union Cemetery between Hudson Falls and Fort Edward, where his ancient tombstone now has the protection of a high iron fence, and in 1925 when a monument to the Black Watch and its Major was unveiled at Fort Ticonderoga. Both occasions were under the auspices of the St. Andrews Society of Scots of Glens Falls and vicinity, and the New York State Historical Association.

Of all the new material which has been found since 1910 none is so important or so interesting as the following letter from Major Duncan Campbell of Inverawe:

Albany, 14th March, 1758.

Dear Sir,

I received your letter from Inveraw of the 25th November and the first from you since we parted, tho I have been informed by letters that come to hand, of your writing formerly. The State you sent me of my affairs is not very agreeable nor encouraging for me to make a retreat that I had in view, and in a little time I believe might be in my power but I am not disappointed; and notwithstanding I shall do all in my power to assist you. I am sorry that no other scheme of living can be accomplished upon the fund, than the one fixed on; to me it gives uneasinefs of minde, tho I'm sensible the consequence may be worse if it is not followed, and therefore bear it with concern. I don't choose to mention my reasons or enter upon particulars as letters from this part of the world to yours are lyable to inspection and many accidents. I see a separation must be that will expose them to the disrespect and ridicule of many; coud they live together in the way proposed it might prevent much of that but I can't hope or expect it from what I know.

As to my advice or directions with regard to any plan you, and my other freinds, to whom I fear I have given much trouble and to whom in any event I shall rekon myself oblig'd there is no sort of use for them, you are best judges, and as I am well satisfied that everything will be don and ordered for the best, I shall be as satisfied with any consequence. I am glade you think of raising nurseries and planting, I sent from this Country to be forwarded by Mr. Gatty from Belfast two Barrels of the different kindes of

OLD INVERAWE HOUSE

Photo by Miss Dorothea E. Seaton, Edinburgh

Showing Door to Ghost Room from Balcony in En-   Entrance Hall (Door to Ghost Room may be seen in
trance Hall   upper left hand corner)

Timber tree seeds &c. but I doubt they will be too late excepting the Pines which seed will do when two year old.

Your letter came a few days ago by an advice Ship of War, which superceeded My Lord Loudoun in the Command and General Abercrombie appointed in his place, with many other changes and promotions in our Military affairs in this Continent, how far they may change our Luck I shall not pretend to judge, but we have need of some sort of medicine for that end. We have a prospect of a very warm and vigorous campaign, and I hope it will be suc- cefsful. Our Regiment is appointed for the Lewisburgh Expedition, but as we are so far up in the Country where the Generall is to have his department and opperations it is yet uncertain but he may keep us with him; we are all in very good health and compleat for service.

I cannot yet know what remittance I can make for this year, some I will and shall, sometime before we take the field or the midle of May. To prevent a relaps of my last years companion I travelled to the Southard during the severity of the winter to N. York and Philadelfia &c. which have had the desyrd effect and I'm now as chois as ever, but it will not enlarge the remittance.

I have had no letter from Sandy Campbell since Aprile last, Nor from Jesie since July, I received one from Mr. Richardson with yours which I shall answer by next Pacquett and tell him so with my compliments. Lykways please tell Peter Campbell that his letter came at the same time, and that as Adam Fisher is here I had ane opportunity of enquiring about his son who is at present out as master, not Capt. of a Privateer there was no such prizes or Fortoune as Peter believed what may be now I know not but there is no great prospect of it. This is the only letter I write by the first Pacquett, so that you may communicate it to my friends as a proof of my being well and youll in the same course make my compliments to them all.

I'm sorry that Captain Campbell should make objections to the payment of his Bill; he brought me 3   for which I cleared him all his charge and gav   at that time 20 guineas over for his own trouble   expense this he knows and will appear by my   which you can see;   this indeed I thought suitable any expense he coud incur in Mull and that it   my power to give him or not the raising of an   rather than have any difference about it let h   what I had allowed me by the Regiment which was £3 per man for the first two years and two guineas for the remaining years that at a medium or the full as you please but I hope he'll allow interest upon what Ballance may be due by him upon such an amot from the time it fell due April 46 when he went to the Regt.

I am, ...

My dear Sir,

Your affect. humble servant.

Dun. Campbell.

To

John Campbell of Cloichombie Esqr.

Inveraray,

North Brittain.

(edge of letter torn off—hence gaps) (J.FC.)

The letter bears the Inverawe arms on seal and is endorsed, probably by the addressee "14th March 1758, from Inveraw concerning his familie and affairs and Lieut. Collonel Dugd. Campbell's Bill."

This letter will bear reading and re-reading. The first and to the writer the most important part of the letter was some financial and family problem. Unfortunately his guarded and cryptic message caused by the fear that the letter might be opened by another than the addressee will perhaps leave it always an unsolved mystery. It would be interesting to know what success attended the planting of the two barrels of timber seed. His guess that the Black Watch might be used in the Ticonderoga campaign rather than the Lewisburgh as planned, proved correct. It would be interesting to know what the malady of the previous winter was, to prevent a relapse of which it had been necessary to travel to the Southard. The letter closes with another financial problem. If he means that he was allowed ten or fifteen dollars per man for the thousand men in the Regiment, that would be a very sizable income for those days and the bill must have been a large one. The allowance, however, might have been for recruits secured or some other regimental activity. But aside from the interesting contents of this letter its real value is that it gives an opportunity to learn something of the character of its writer. One can read between the lines that Duncan of Inverawe was a reserved man of a strong but a quiet, kindly nature, he would suffer loss himself rather than make trouble for others, and after having done his best was willing to take whatever came without complaint. It quite matches the Inverawe of the ghost story who promised to protect a fugitive and then stood by his

The Black Watch of Canada at the dedication of the Black Watch Memorial Tablet July 8, 1925, the inscription of which reads:

A. D. 1925. The Saint Andrews Society of Glens Falls, N. Y., erected this tablet to commemorate the heroic gallantry of the 42nd Regiment of Foot, better known as "The Royal Highlanders" or "THE BLACK WATCH" who on July 8, 1758, lost here in killed and wounded over six hundred of the thousand men engaged. Mortally wounded on that day was their Major, DUNCAN CAMPBELL OF INVERAWE, the hero of one of the most noted ghost stories of Scottish history and of Robert Louis Stevenson's poem, "Ticonderoga."

oath even though the refugee was the murderer of his cousin. The reader of this letter can not help but feel drawn towards its writer.

Now what was the immediate family and what was the background of our hero. One version of the ghost story was that he made his will the night before the battle, but no sensible man waits until death is at the door for this very important transaction and we find the following in Vol. XV, Abstract of Entry in Sheriff Court Books of Argyll at Inveraray.

"Disposition by Major Duncan Campbell of Inverawe to Lieut. Dugald Campbell, his eldest son procreated between him and Mrs. Jean Campbell, his wife, whom, failing, to Lieut. Alexander Campbell, his second son, whom failing, Duncan Campbell, his third and youngest son, whom failing, to any other sons he may lawfully have, and the heirs male of their bodies in succession, whom failing, to Janet Campbell, his only daughter now in life procreated between him and the said Mrs. Jean Campbell, of his whole lands and estate of Inverawe and others, under certain reservations; dated at Glasgow 17th April, 1756; witnesses, John Campbell of Cloichombie, Alexander Campbell in Achalion, and others."

This establishes Inverawe's family and we will see what became of them. Dugald was appointed 2nd Lieutenant in the 21st or Royal North British Fuziliers, December 28, 1755, joined his Regiment at Gibraltar in 1756, died and was succeeded by John Wallace, March 1st, 1758.

Alexander was appointed Lieutenant in the Black Watch Jan. 28, 1756, was wounded at Ticonderoga and invalided to Glasgow where he was promoted to a Captaincy in the Argyllshire Regiment of Fencible men, July 21, 1759, died unmarried Feb. 8, 1760 and was buried in Grey Friers Burying Ground. A powder horn said to have belonged to Lt. Alexander and bearing the coat-of-arms of the Campbells of Inverawe is at the McCord Museum of McGill University in Montreal.

Duncan, third son of Inverawe, is still a mystery but the fact that Janet was proven heir to Inverawe February 5, 1762 would seem to show that he had died without issue before that date.

Major Duncan, born Nov. 22, 1702, married March 20, 1732 Jean, daughter of Col. Alexander Campbell of Finab. She died at Edinburgh August 20, 1761. When Janet succeeded to Inverawe in 1762 therefore her father, her mother and three brothers had all predeceased her—a tragic mortality in six short years. There is a family tradition that Major Duncan mortgaged Inverawe to his brother-in-law, Col. Robert Campbell of Finab and Monzie and that according to old Scottish law the property was handed over to the man who advanced the money until the rental had paid off the debt, and that this arrangement was called a wadset. Whether Col. Campbell of Finab and Monzie acquired the property by wadset or purchase, it passed into his hands soon after Janet proved her title and it is said that when she left the estate she washed her hands in a bottle of wine at the border, which we were told was an old Highland custom. The owner of Inverawe in 1910 was a descendant of Col. Robert Campbell of Finab and Monzie, a Mrs. Campbell of Dunstaffnage. Since then we are informed it was purchased by the late Mr. James Currie and is now for sale to settle his estate.

Janet who married Capt. William Pitman, had only one daughter, Susan, who died unmarried. So with her the descendants of Major Duncan Campbell of Inverawe are at an end.

There is a very interesting tale about an Inverawe cup. It seems that in 1714 the three brothers, Archibald of Inverawe, Dugald of Shirvan, and Alexander of Kilmartin, each got a silver cup. The Kilmartins always kept their cup but both those of Inverawe and Shirvan were lost. This was such a grief to the Inverawes that the fact was often mentioned. On one occasion a friend who had heard of this cup was hunting in Ireland and stopped at a wretched little inn to get a drink for himself and his horse. The place was so disreputable looking that he would not go in but had his drink brought out to him. It came in a battered old metal cup and on the chance that it might be of value, he bought it from the landlord. To his great pleasure he found on having it cleaned that it was the long lost Inverawe cup. He had an inscription put on it, recording the finding, and sent it to Archibald Campbell of Blackhouse, a nephew of Major Duncan, and the representative at that time of the Inverawe family. The cup is still a treasured possession of the descendants of this Archibald, the Campbells of Arduaine, Lochgilphead.

—From "Auchindarroch Miscellany"

THE INVERAWE CUP

THE BLACK WATCH AT TICONDEROGA

The will of the Archibald of Inverawe of the Silver Cup and father of Major Duncan Campbell, is as follows:

"1727, February 23rd—Disposition by Archibald Campbell of Inveraw to Duncan Campbell, his eldest lawful son, and the heirs male of his body, whom failing, to Dugall Campbell, his second lawful son, and his heirs male, whom failing, Lachlan Campbell, his third son, and Alexander Campbell, his fourth son, whom all failing, the heirs of the Granter and Janet McLean, his spouse, whom failing, his heirs of any other marriage of his lands of Inveraw, Drumchoise, Dalneass, etc., with certain exceptions, including a life rent right granted by the deceased Archibald Campbell of Inveraw to Lilias Campbell, his spouse, now spouse to Angus Campbell of Dunstagnage; dated at Inveraw 14th February 1722."

Another interesting fact in the Inverawe annals is that Dugald Campbell of London in the parish of Saint Martin's, Westminster, and County of Middlesex, by his will bearing date the 2nd day of June 1718, gave to old decayed men and young women of Campbell of Inverawe's family, the sum of £300, and that this "Inverawe Annuity Fund" since augmented, is still administered by Trustees chosen from the Inverawe heirs.

The present known Campbells who are proud to claim that they are of the Clan Inverawe are descended from Alexander, brother of Duncan, the fourth son of Archibald, as named in the foregoing will. Alexander was born in 1710 and married Ann Somerville in 1747. If all of the descendants of this union have been of as fine, high character as those whom we have been privileged to meet, the world has indeed been richer for the Campbells of Inverawe.

Family Tree of The Campbells of Inverawe

The family does not seem to be entirely in agreement on the line back of the 18th Century. The following is gathered from different branches. One version is that the Inverawes descended from Sir Archibald Campbell of Lochow, whose son Colin was knighted by Alexander III, 1280, and died 1294. His son, Niel or Nigel of Lochow, died 1360, and *his* son, Dugald or Duncan was the 1st "Inverawe" and ancestor of the Clan Dhonnachie Campbells. He got a grant of the estate of Inveraw and Cruachan from David II, 1330. A later Inveraw got a grant of lands from Queen Mary,

1558. With the exception of a gap of about 60 years from 1460 or so to 1510, we have a complete record of "Inveraws" practically an unbroken succession from father to son.

Another version is the following:

Archibald, c/v from 1st Earl of Argyll

Dougal, c/v 22.11.1485, from 2nd Earl. Sasine Des. 1486. Officer of Over Lochow to the Earl. (Inverawe deeds)

Archibald, signs Archibald McCoul McConachie of Inverawe 1519, (Thanes of Cawdor), c/v from 2nd Earl as heir to Dugal (Inverawe deeds) married Margaret Campbell.

Dougal, (Inverawe 1548-1562). (Register of Decreets and Acts) said to have married a dau. of Lochnell.

Archibald, (1562-1567 or 1576) married Margaret C. dau. of Dougal C. of Ardcullour, sister of Sir James C. VIth of Ardkinklas. (A. Charters)

Dougal, (1576 or 1567-1583) married Christian Carswell, dau. (or granddaughter) of Bishop Carswell. Relict of Dougal 1587. She afterward married Neill Campbell, Bishop of Lismore.

Archibald, (1583-1650)

Dougal, (1650-1674), burned "Bonnie House of Airlie" 1640. married 1st, Agnes, dau. of Sir Robert C. of Glenarguhy (Braedalbane) 2nd, Janet, dau. of Rory McNeill of Barra.

Archibald, (1674-1705), son of Dougal and Agnes. Married 1st, Mary, dau. of Hector McNeill of Thayneis. 2nd, Lilias, dau. of Sir James C. of Lawers.

Archibald, (1705-1730) married Janet McLean of Torloisk. Served heir to Cattinis 1700, later Inverawe, etc. Received Inverawe cup 1714.

Duncan (1730-1758), Major Black Watch, married Jane Campbell of Finab.

ARCHIBALD OF INVERAWE
b. abt. 1670. got cup 1714. d. 1730.
m. Janet Maclean of Tarloisk, in Mull, abt. 1700.

Duncan of Inveraw Maj. Black Watch b. 1702. d. 1758 m. Jean Campbell of Finab	Barbara b. 1703 Campbell m. Archd. of Jura	Archibald b. 1705 d. before 1721	Dugald b. 1706 no issue	Alexander b. 1710 m. 1747 Ann Somer- ville	-Lachlan b. 1709 d. young -Isobel b. 1711 -Elizabeth b. 1713 -Patrick b. 1714 -Lilias b. 1716 -Ann b. 1717 -John b. 1719

Dugald Lieut. d. unm.	Alexander b. abt. 1705 Lieut. Black Watch. d. of wounds rec'd Ticongeroga. Unm.	Duncan Lieut. d. unm.	Janet m. Wm. Pitman, M. D. 33d Regt. (Duke of Cumberland's army. Sold Inveraw 1762 to her uncle, Col. Robt. Campbell of Monzie and Finab. One dau. Susan, d unm.

Jean m. Duncan Campbell Achlian	John	Archibald of Blackhouse m. Katherine Fish 1817	Ann d. unm.	Alexander	Duncan b. 1763 d. 1815 m. 1798 Harriot Young, b. 1774.

Alexander of Auchindarock
Pur'd 1829. Trustee sold
Tirvine to James A. C. 1830.
3rd Dragoon Guards. d. July 1902.
m. Harriet Keir, dau. Sir James Keir.

See next page

Archibald b. 1842 d. Aug. 1885 74th Highlanders m. Isabella C., dau. Col. Fairlie of Coodham A.	Julia	Mary	Alister b. 1846. Killed Sakokunis Krael 1879. (Schipka pass Campbell)	James Arthur b. 1850 d. Nov. 1929 m. Miss E. M. Bruce	Walter b. 1854	Neil b. 1858 m. M. G. Bovill

Arduaine family

Alister Magnus of Auchindarroch b. 1868. d. Aug. 1930 m. 1st, Lilias Mary 1897 dau. Robt. Roberston of Mountgrenan, Glasgow	Roma	Constance 1870	Archibald b. 1878 m. Eva, dau Col. Agnew East Warristoone	Zella Muriel b. 1880 m. Robertson Glasgow	Donald b. 1881 d. 1886

Alister Norman b. 1898	Colin C.

m. 2nd Evelyn Sanderson 1903, Edinburgh

Amy Muriel 1905	Neil Arch'd b. 1906, d. 1907	Alan Keir b. 1908

DUNCAN (son of Alexander who was brother of Duncan of Inveraw)
b. 1763   d. 1815   m. 1798   Harriot Young, b. 1774

Henrietta	Alexander	Robert	Ann	Duncan	Jane	James Archibald
b. 1800	b. 1801	b. 1802	Eliza	b. 1805	b. 1806	b. 1807, d. 1879
m. Rev. Bracken			b. 1803	d. at Eton	m. Sir Alex. Spearman.	m. 1st 1832 Jane Augusta Pocklington d. 1842 m. 2nd Maria
Henrietta Eliza d. unm.						

Jane	Henrietta	Augusta	Alex.	Edmund	Horace	Grace Cameron d. 1906

Rudolph

Thos. Edmund	Augustus
b. 1809	b. 1811
m. Henrietta	d. young in
du Chesne	snow storm
St. Hilaire	in Alps.
Canada	

Edmund	Archibald	Jucherau	Bruce	Laura	Robert	Duncan	Donald	Colin
b. 1843	d. 1899			Hermoine				m.
m. Nellie Lind				d.				Mabel G. Allen

Duncan	Archie	Charles	Lola
killed in war			

Edmund	Bruce	Hugh	Etta
	killed in war		

Enid	Phoebe	Colin d.

JAMES ARCHIBALD (son of Duncan, son of Alexander bro. of Duncan of
    Inveraw.
  b. 1807 d. 1879
  m. 1st 1832 Jane Augusta Pocklington, d. 1842

Jane Eliza	Laura	Duncan	Edmund	Alex'r	Florence	Lorne Augustus
b. 1833	Beatrice	Pocklington	d. 1887	Elizabeth	b. 1842
d. 1924	b. 1834	d. unm.	m. Margaret	d. unm.	d. 1893
m. Rev. Walter	d. 1917		Campbell		m. 1875
Tait. Min of	unm.		d. 1909		Cecelia Martin
St. Madoes, Perthshire					d. 1898
b. 1836 d. 1905					

		Maria	Duncan	Edmund	Lorne	Ronald	James
		Grace	McIver	Alex'r	Francis	Bruce	Arch'd
J. H. M.	Adam	m. 1904			d.	m. 1911	m. Bessie
(Minna)	Duncan	Louis Carey				May	Anderson
	m. 1901					Brockman	
	Evelyn Heath						

			Estella Grace		Bruce	Neill
			and Patricia		b. 1912	b. 1924
Barbara	Ian Ford	Duncan				
Jean	b. 1904					

John	Frances	Patrick
Anderson		

Ethel	Frederick	Cecil	Audrey	Ian
m. 1897			d. 1918	
Chas. Desborough			O. A. S.	

Jan	Joyce	Peter

James Archibald (b. 1807, d. 1879)
m. 2nd Maria Grace Cemeron, d. 1906

Grace	Donald	Henrietta	James	Maria	Lilias	Mabel
m. Dr.	Charles	d. 1860	Archibald	Josephine	MacDonald	Harriott
Neill	d. 1923			m. 1887		m. 1887
				d. 1888		Hugh Daubney
John				Rev. Reginald Letts		Lieut. RN
m.						d. 1914

Christian Francis

b. 1888

Gladys	Marjory	Hugh
M. W. L.		b. 1900
Mellersh		

Mary	John	Veronica

Dugal John	Evan Cameron
m.	m. Marie

APPENDIX

A

ROLL FROM AN OLD PAPER IN POSSESSION OF THE 7TH DUKE OF ATHOLL. OFFICERS OF THE 42ND HIGHLANDERS, NEW YORK, MAY 22, 1757.

Lt. Col. Francis Grant, son of the Laird of Grant, wounded at Ticonderoga.

Major Duncan Campbell, of Inverawe, killed at Ticonderoga.

Captain Gordon Graham, of Drainie, wounded at Ticonderoga.

Captain John Reid, of Straloch, wounded at Martinique.

Captain John NcNeil.

Captain Allan Campbell, son of Barcaldine.

Captain Thomas Graeme, of Duchray, wounded at Ticonderoga.

Captain James Abercrombie.

Captain John Campbell, of Strachur, wounded at Ticonderoga.

Captain John Campbell, of Duneavis, killed at Ticonderoga.

Lieutenant William Grant, of Rothiemurchus family, wounded at Ticonderoga.

Lieutenant Robert Gray, wounded at Ticonderoga.

Lieutenant John Campbell, younger of Glenyon, wounded at Ticonderoga.[1]

Lieutenant George Farquharson, son of Farquharson of Micris, Braemar, killed at Ticonderoga.

Lieutenant Sir James Cockburn.[2]

Lieutenant Kenneth Tolmie.

Lieutenant James Grant (Adjutant), wounded at Ticonderoga.

Lieutenant John Graham (quartermaster) wounded at Ticonderoga and wounded at Fort Pitt.

Lieutenant Hugh McPherson, killed at Ticonderoga.

---

1. Major Sir Duncan Campbell of Bacaldine says should be "of Glendaruel' and that younger of Glenlyon went to the Marines in 1755.

2. Lieut. Sir James Cockburn transferred to 48th Foot. Ensign Patrick Balneavis made Lieut., commission dated 1st April, 1758, and Mr. Elbert Hering succeeded to the Ensigncy, commission dated April 3d, 1758. (See extract from letter Jas. Abercrombie to Lord Viscount Barrington, Albany, May 27, 1758.)

Blair Castle at Blair Atholl   Reviewing the Atholl Highlanders

Sir John James Hugh Henry Stewart-Murray, K. T., Seventh Duke
of Atholl

Lieutenant Alex. Turnbull, of Strathcavers, wounded at Martinique.

Lieutenant Alex. Campbell, son of Inverawe, wounded at Ticonderoga.

Lieutenant Alex. McIntosh, wounded at Ticonderoga.

Lieutenant James Gray.

Lieutenant William Baillie, killed at Ticonderoga.

Lieutenant Hugh Arnot.

Lieutenant John Sutherland, killed at Ticonderoga.

Lieutenant John Small.

Lieutenant Archibald Campbell.

Lieutenant James Campbell.

Lieutenant Archibald Lamont.

Ensign Duncan Campbell, wounded at Fort Pitt.

Ensign Patrick Balneavis,[1] son of Edradour, wounded at Ticonderoga, wounded at Martinique.

Ensign Patrick Stewart,[2] son of Bonskeid, killed at Ticonderoga.

Ensign Norman MacLeod.

Ensign George Campbell.

Ensign Donald Campbell.

Ensign James McIntosh, wounded at Fort Pitt.

Ensign Alex. McIntosh, wounded at Martinique.

Ensign Peter Grant, wounded at Ticonderoga.

Three additional Companies embarked for America, November, 1757.

Captain James Stewart, younger of Urrard, wounded at Ticonderoga.

Captain James Murray, son of Lord G. Murray, wounded at Ticonderoga, wounded at Martinique.

Captain Thomas Stirling, younger of Ardoch, wounded at Martinique, wounded at New Jersey.

Lieutenant Simon Blair.

Lieutenant David Barclay, killed at Martinique.

Lieutenant Archibald Campbell, wounded at Ticonderoga.

Lieutenant Alex. Mackay.

Lieutenant Alex. Menzies.

---

1. See Foot Note at bottom of preceding page.
2. Miss Ethel Lomas, copyist at Public Record Office, London, is authority for the statement that this should be Peter (not Patrick) Stewart.

Lieutenant David Milne,[3] wounded at Ticonderoga, wounded at Martinique.

Ensign Duncan Stewart, son of Derculich.

Ensign George Rattray, son of Dalralzion, killed at Ticonderoga.

Ensign Alex. Farquharson.

"Ensign John Smith is added in ink to the 1858 Army List in the N. Y. State Library at Albany and is also marked as "wounded at Ticonderoga."
3. This name is given as David Mills in the Army List, but the Duke of Atholl is authority for the statement that Milne is correct.

B

ROLL OF CAPT. JOHN REID'S COMPANY, NOV. 1757.

The following is the roll of Capt. John Reid's Company of the 42nd, which was commanded by Capt. James Murray during the expedition. Taken from Atholl Records, page 440, Vol. III.

Capt. James Murray, wounded.
Lieut. Kenneth Tolmie.
Lieut. David Mill, wounded.
Ensign Charles Menzies.
Sergt. James McNab.
Sergt. John McAndrews.
Sergt. John Watson.

Sergt. Alex'r Cumming.
Corporal John Cumming.
Corporal Jonathan Grant.
Corporal Angus McDonald.
Corporal John Stewart.
Drum Walter McIntyre, killed.
Drum Alan Campbell.

Privates

Wm. Anderson.
John Buchanan, killed.
Angus Cameron.
Hugh Cameron, killed.
Wm. Carmichael.
Donald Carr, killed.
Hugh Christie.
Alex. Cumming.
James Farquharson, killed.
Alex Fraser.
Donald Fraser.
Donald Fraser.

James McIntyre, killed.
Hector McInven.
Hugh McKay.
Alex'r McKenzie.
Hugh McKenzie.
John McKenzie, killed.
John McKenzie.
Roderick McKenzie.
Dougall McLachlan, killed.
John McLaren.
Roderick McLaren.
Neil McLeod.

Hugh Fraser.
Hugh Fraser, killed.
John Forbes.
John Graham.
Donald Grant.
James Grant.
John Grant.
John Grant.
William Grant.
James Gordon.
William Gordon.
Donald Kennedy.
Donald Kennedy.
John Kennedy.
George McAdam.
John McArthur.
Donald McColl.
Donald McDiarmid.
Angus McDonald.
Arch'd McDonald.
Arch'd McDonald, killed.
James McDonald, killed.
John McDonald.
Lachlan McDonald.
William McDonald, killed.
Neil McEachern.
Peter McFarlane.
Peter McFarlane, killed.
John McGillvray.
Leonard McGlashan.
Alex McGregor.
Donald McGregor.
Robert McGregor.
John McIntosh.
Alex McIntyre.
Donald McIntyre.

Norman McLeod, killed.
Donald McLeish.
Donald McLeish.
William McLinnion.
Neil McMillan.
Donald McNeil, killed.
Neil McNeil.
Hugh McPhee.
John McPhee.
Alex McPherson.
Donald McPherson.
Donald McQueen, killed.
James Michael.
Donald Murray.
James Murray.
James Rea.
Alex'r Reid.
Alex'r Ross.
Donald Ross.
Hugh Ross, killed.
John Ross.
Donald Robertson.
Neil Shaw.
John Sinclair, died of wounds.
John Smith.
Walter Spaulding.
Alex'r Stewart.
Charles Stewart, died of wounds.
Donald Stewart, died of wounds.
Walter Stewart, died of wounds .
Robert Urquhart.
Donald Watson.
Donald Wheet.
William Wishart.
Duncan Wright.

The above roll was made out at the muster in October, 1757, and contains the names of those who served in the Company for the previous six months. Unfortunately the names of the non-commissioned officers and men who were wounded at Ticonderoga are not shown.

C

ROLL OF CAPT. JAMES MURRAY'S COMPANY, NOV. 1757.

This Company was at Fort Edward captained by Capt. James Abercrombie and not in the battle of July 8, 1758.

Atholl Records, p. 431, Vol. III.

Sergt. Wm. Grant.   Corporal John Leslie.
Sergt. Charles Robinson.   Corporal Robert Lachlan.
Sergt, John McQueen.   Drummer Alan Campbell.

Privates

George Bremmer.   Thos. McNab.
Donald Brown.   Alex McPherson.
Duncan Cameron.   James McPherson.
John Campbell.   Donald McRaw.
Donald Conacher.   Robert Menzies.
William Cowie.   William Munroe.
James Douglas.   John Murray.
Donald Drummond.   Alex'r Nicholson.
James Duncan.   Alex'r Norrie.
Alex Fraser (1).   Alex'r Reid.
Alex Fraser (2).   Alex'r Robertson.
William Fife.   Angus Robertson.
Robert Grant.   Archibald Robertson.
Alex Irvine.   Charles Robertson.
James Kennedy.   Donald Robertson.
Duncan McAndrew.   James Robertson.
Donald McDiarmid.   James Robertson.
Archibald McDonald.   John Robertson.
Archibald McDonald.   Peter Robertson.
Donald McDonald.   James Scroggie.
John McDonald.   Alex'r Stewart.
William McDonald.   Alex'r Stewart.

Peter McFarlane.
Alex'r McIntosh.
Robert McIntosh.
Robert McIntosh.
William McIntosh.
Donald McLean.
Donald McLean.

Alex'r Stewart.
John Stewart.
Robert Stewart.
Thomas Stewart.
William Stewart.
John Wighton.
John Wighton.

D

LIST OF PROMOTION 42D REGIMENT OF FOOT.

From Paper in Public Record Office, London.

RANK	NAME	DATE 1758	IN ROOM OF
Major	Gordon Graham	17th July	Duncan Campbell, dead
Captain	William Grant	23d "	Gordon Graham, promoted
Capt. Lieut.	Robert Gray	22d "	John Campbell, killed
Lieut.	Duncan Campbell	23d "	William Grant, promoted
"	Donald Campbell	24th "	Robert Gray, promoted
"	James McIntosh	25th "	George Farquharson, killed
"	John Smith	26th "	Hugh McPherson, killed
"	Peter Grant	27th "	William Baillie, killed
"	Duncan Stewart	28th "	John Sutherland, killed
"	Alex. Farquharson	29th "	Hugh Arnotte, pref'd (80th foot)
Ensign	Arch. Campbell, Jr.	21st "	Norman McLeod, pref'd (80th foot)
"	John Gregor	22nd "	George Campbell, pref'd (80th foot)
"	Lewis Grant	23d "	Patrick Stewart, killed
"	Arch. Campbell, Sen'r	24th "	George Ratthray, killed
"	John Graham	25th "	Duncan Campbell, promoted
"	Allen Grant	26th "	Donald Campbell, promoted
"	John Leith	27th "	Jas. McIntosh, promoted
"	Charles Menzies	28th "	John Smith, promoted
"	Archibald McNab	29th "	Peter Grant, promoted

E

COMPARISON OF LOSSES OF BLACK WATCH AT TICONDEROGA WITH THOSE OF OTHER WARS.

In the "Regimental Losses in the American Civil War, 1861, 1865. A treatise in the extent and nature of the mortuary losses in the Union Regiments, with full and exhaustive statistics compiled from the official records on file on the State Military Bureaus and at Washington, by William F. Fox, Lieut. Col. U. S. V., president of the Society of the 12th Army Corps; late president of the 107th New York Veteran Volunteer Association. Albany Publishing Company, Albany, N. Y., 1899." The writer states that he has examined the records of 2,000 regiments of the Union Army and on page 2 he says, "The one regiment in all the Union Army which sustained the greatest loss in battle during the American Civil War was the 5th New Hampshire Infantry. It lost 295 men, killed or mortally wounded in action during the four years of service from 1861 to 1865. It served in the first division, second corps. This division was commanded successively by General Richardson, Hancock, Caldwall, Barlow and Miles and any regiment that followed the fortunes of these men was sure to find plenty of bloody work cut out for it. Its loss includes 18 officers killed, a number far in excess of the usual proportions and indicates that the men were bravely led."

"There were 34 regiments of the Union Army whose casualties in killed, wounded or missing amounted to 58 per cent or over of the men engaged in one battle in each case, however, there was not a full regiment engaged. For example, the 1st Minnesota at Gettysburg, which was the highest per centage, had 47 killed and 168 wounded, or a total loss of 215 out of 262 men engaged. This is a loss of 82 per cent.

The 9th Illinois at Shiloh had 61 killed, 300 wounded and 5 missing, a total of 63.3 per cent.

The Light Brigade which has been immortalized by Tennyson took 673 officers and men into that charge at Balaklava in which 113 were killed and 134 wounded, a total of 247 or 36.7 per cent.

Lord Howe's Monument in Westminster Abbey

The heaviest loss in the German army of the Franco-Prussian war was the 16th Infantry (3d Westphalian) at Mars LaTour which had 509 killed, 619 wounded, 365 missing, a total of 1,484 or 49.4 per cent. out of 3,000 men. The regiments of the German army had 3,000 men."

The above are the greatest casualties suffered in three great wars taken from a book compiled by an authority who had made a study of the subject. Compare with these the loss of the Black Watch at Ticonderoga given by Col. Stewart of Garth as 8 officers, 9 sergeants and 297 men killed and 17 officers, 10 sergeants and 306 soldiers wounded or a casualty of 647 (64.7 per cent) out of the 1,000 men of the 42nd reported by General Abercrombie at Lake George, June 29, 1758.

F

TABLE OF LOSSES OF BLACK WATCH IN SEVEN YEAR WAR.

The loss sustained by the regiment during the seven years it was employed in America and the West Indies was as follows:

	KILLED						WOUNDED					
	Field Officers	Captains	Subalterns	Serjeants	Drummers	Privates	Field Officers	Captains	Subalterns	Serjeants	Drummers	Privates
Ticonderoga, July 8, 1758	1	1	6	9	2	297		5	12	10		306
Martinique, January, 1759						8			1	2		22
Gaudeloupe, Feb. and Mar., 1759		1	1			25			4	3		57
General Amherst's Expedition to the Lakes, July and Aug., 1759						3				1		4
Martinique, Jan. and Feb., 1762	1	1	6			12	1	1	7	3	1	72
Havana, June and July, 1762, both battalions						6				1		12
Expedition under Colonel Boquet,, August, 1763	1	1	1			26	1	1		2	2	30
Second Expedition under Boquet, in 1764 and 1765						7				1		19
Total in the Seven Years' War	1	3	9	12	2	384	1	7	25	22	4	522

Stewart of Garth, Appendix.

G
OFFICIAL TITLES OF BLACK WATCH AT DIFFERENT PERIODS.

1667 to 1739, The Black Watch.

1739 to 1749, The Regiment was known during this period by the names of its Colonels, as was the custom in the British Army at that time, Earl of Crawford's, Lord Sempill's, Lord John Murray's. It was also called The Highland Regiment. It is said that the Regiment was at first the 43d Regt. of Foot, but while it was 43d in order of precedence it is a question if it was ever officially called the 43d.

1749 to 1758, 42nd Regiment of Foot (The Highland Regiment).

1758 to 1861, 42nd (or Royal Highland) Regiment of Foot.

1861 to 1881, 42nd Royal Highlanders (The Black Watch).

1881 to date, 1st Battalion The Black Watch (Royal Highlanders).

1758 to 1786, 2nd Battalion 42nd (or Royal Highland), Regiment of Foot.

1786 to 1862, 73d (Highland) Regiment of Foot.

1862 to 1881, 73d (Perthshire) Regiment of Foot.

1881 to date, 2nd Battalion The Black Watch (Royal Highlanders).

PRINCIPAL CAMPAIGNS, BATTLES, ETC.

* "Honors" on the Colors, the figures showing the Battalion concerned.

1743-47 Flanders.	1801 Mandora.
1745 Fontenoy.	*1808-14 Peninsula (1).
1745 Jacobite rising.	1808 Roleia.
1757-60 Canada.	1808 Vimiera.
1758 Ticonderoga.	*1809 Corunna (1).
1759 Guadeloupe.	1810 Busaco.
1762 Martinique.	*1811 Fuentes d'Onor (1).

1762 Havannah.
1762-67 Indian Frontier.
1763 Bushy Run.
1775-81 America.
1776 Long Island.
1776 White Plains.
1776 Brooklyn.
1776 Fort Washington.
1777 Pisquata.
1777 Brandywine.
1777 Germantown.
1778 Freehold.
1780 Charlestown.
*1783 Mysore (2).
*1783 Mangalore (2).
1793 Pondicherry.
1893-95 Flanders.
1793 Nieuport.
1794 Nimeguen.
1795 Ceylon.
1795 Guildermalsen.
1796 St. Lucia.
1797 St. Vincent.
1798 Minorca.
*1799 Seringapatam (2)
1799 Genoa.
1799 Cadiz.
1800 Malta.
*1801 Egypt (1).
1801 Alexandria.
1801 Aboukir.

1812 Ciudad Rodrigo.
1812 Salamanca.
1812 Burgos.
*1813 Pyrenees (1).
1813 Gohrde.
*1813 Nivelle (1).
*1813 Nive (1).
*1814 Orthes (1).
1814 Antwerp.
*1814 Toulouse (1).
1815 Quatre Bras.
*1815 Waterloo (1 and 2)
1815 Netherlands.
*1846-53 South Africa (2).
*1854 Alma (1).
1854 Balaclava.
1854 Kertch.
1855 Yenikale.
*1855 Sevastopol (1).
1857-58 Indian Mutiny.
1857 Cawnpore.
*1858 Lucknow (1).
*1874 Ashantee (1).
*1882-84 Egypt (1).
*1882 Tel-el-Kebir (1).
*1884-85 Nile (1).
1884 El-Teb.
1884 Tamai.
*1885 Kirbekan (1).
*1899-1902 South Africa.
*1900 Paardeberg.

H

BRITISH REGIMENTS AT TICONDEROGA, 1758

With Notes From Farmer's Regimental Records.

27th.

1751-1881, The 27th (Inniskilling) Regiment of Foot. Also 1758 "Lord Blakeney's."

1881 (from) First Battalion "The Royal Inniskilling Fusiliers."

Nickname—"The Lumps."

Notes.—Formed from three Companies of the Inniskilling forces. It is unique in using the old Irish war-pipes. While employed on the Isthmus of Darien all but nine of six hundred men succumbed. For distinguished gallantry at St. Lucia, in 1696, it was directed that the French garrison in marching out should lay down their arms to the 27th, other marks of favor being likewise accorded to the officers and men of the regiment.

42nd.

1749-58, 42nd Regiment of Foot (The Highland Regiment).

1758-1861, 42nd (or Royal Highland) Regiment of Foot. Also "Lord John Murray's," 1758 and 59.

1881 (from) 1st Battalion The Black Watch (Royal Highlanders).

Regimental Badges—"The Royal Cypher within the Garter." The badge and motto of the Order of the Thistle. Also (in each of the four corners) the Royal Cypher ensigned with the Imperial Crown. Also "The Spinx" (for Egypt, 1801).

Notes.—The 1st Battalion of this famous corps, the oldest Highland regiment in the British army, was raised from six independent companies of Highlanders. Its sombre dress of black, blue, and green tartan gave rise to its popular name. To enumerate its services is simply to narrate the military history of Great Britain since the early part of the last century. Hardly a campaign has been conducted, or a battle fought, in which the Black Watch—one battalion or the other, or both in company—has not participated; always with bravery, and frequently with conspicuous gallantry. Thereto its records of services abundantly testifies. At Fontenoy, Ticonderoga, and at Bushy Run "extraordinary and unexampled" gallantry was shown. It received Royal distinction in its change of title in 1758, and was privileged to wear the red heckle in the bonnet, in recognition of its conduct at the battle of Guildermalsen in 1795. In Egypt (in 1801, for which it bears "The Sphinx"), before Alexandria, it captured the Standard of the French Invincible Legion. Since then it has heaped fame on fame, and added "honor" to "honor" to its colours. Nor has the 2nd Battalion (raised in Perthshire in 1758 as the second Battalion of the 42nd, but, renumbered, long known as the 73rd prior to the territorial restoration of the ancient status) failed to win fresh laurels as occasion arose. At Mangalore (1783) against Tippoo Sahib, and side by side with the senior Battalion at Waterloo, in the Netherlands, in the Indian Mutiny, and in the Kaffir wars of 1846-53, it has worthily sustained the undying fame of the regiment. Recent events in South Africa show that neither the officers nor the men of today have lost one iota of that traditional dash, determination, and the bravery which have won for the Black Watch so glorious a place in British military annals.

44th.

1751-82, The 44th Regiment of Foot. Also 1758, "General Abercrombie's."

1881 (from) The First Battalion "The Essex Regiment."

Nicknames—"The Two Fours" (of the 44th). "The Little Fighting Fours," (the regiment saw hard service in the Peninsula, and its men were of small average stature). "The Pompadours" and "Saucy Pompeys." (Tradition relates that when the facings were changed in 1764 (the crimson not wearing well) the Colonel desired Blue, but the authorities objecting, he chose Purple, a favorite color of Madame de Pompadour, a mistress of Louis XV, of France).

Notes.—The 44th captured an Eagle of the 62nd French Infantry at Salamanica.

46th

1751-82, The 46th Regiment of Foot. Also 1758 "Lieut. Gen. Thomas Murray's.

1881 (from) Second Battalion "Duke of Cornwall's Light infantry."

Nicknames—These pertain to the late 46th; "Murray's Buck's" (from Colonel name (1743-64) and its smart appearance on home duty in Scottish Royal livery). "The Surprisers" (from an incident (1777) in the American War). "The Lacedemonians" (its Colonel once when under fire, made a disciplinarian speech concerning the Lacedemonians). Also in early days, "The Edinburgh Regiment." "The Red Feathers." "The Docs" (the initials).

Note.—"The Two Feathers" is a distinction of the 46th, a Light company of which, in 1777, with others were brigaded as "The Light Battalion." The Americans were so harrassed by the Brigade that they vowed "No Quarter." In derision, to prevent mistakes, the Light Battalion dyed their feathers red; the 46th Foot alone has retained the distinction.

55th

1757-82, The 55th Regiment of Foot. Also "Lord Howe's" in 1858 and "Prideaux's" in 1759.

1881 (from) Second Battalion "The Border Regiment."

Nickname—"The Two Fives" (to the 55th for its number).

Notes.—The Dragon of China is on the Regimental Badge of the 55th in honor of the victorious campaign in China in 1840-42.

1st and 4th Battalions 60th.

1755-57, The 62nd (Royal American) Regiment of Foot; renumbered.

1757-1824, The 60th (Royal American) Regiment of Foot.

1881 (from) Second Battalion "The Border Regiment."

Notes.—This regiment, though possessing no "Colors," bears more honors than any other regiment, the Highland Light Infantry coming next with twenty-nine. Motto, "Swift and Bold," bestowed according to tradition by General Wolfe in recognition of its conduct at Quebec.

80th.

1758-64, The 80th (Light-armed) Regiment of Foot. Also "Gage's." (Disbanded 1764).

The Royal Regiment of Artillery.

One arm or other of this branch of the Service has, obviously, taken part in every campaign; a particularized list is therefore unnecessary. The guns are the "Colours" of the Artillery, and as such are entitled to all "parade honours." Formerly, regimental honors appear to have been worn by certain companies. Amongst such are "Niagara," "Leipsic," "Waterloo," and "The Dragon of China."

Nicknames—"The Gunners;" "The Four-wheeled Hussars" (of the Royal Horse Artillery).

Notes.—Trains of artillery seem to have been raised in the time of Henry VIII,; and up to 1716 appear to have been disbanded after each campaign. In 1716 several companies received permanent corporate existence, since which exigencies of modern warfare have led to an enormous increase in the number of batteries. But from first to last, the record of the Royal Artillery has been one of distinction, and it may fitly be said to share the honors of all other regiments. The Royal Irish Artillery were absorbed in 1801, and the East India Company's Artillery in 1858.

BRITISH REGIMENTS AT TICONDEROGA, 1759.

1st.

1751-1812, The 1st, or The Royal Regiment of Foot, also the "Royals."

1881 (from) The Royal Scots (Lothian Regiment).

Nickname—"Pontius Pilate's Body-Guard." It is a legend of the Regiment that the Romans carried off a number of wild, war-like Highlanders as prisoners after their conquest of Britain, and these men and their descendants became soldiers of the Roman Empire and as such they guarded the tomb of Our Saviour after the crucifixion. This Scottish company, for it only consisted of one hundred men under a centurion, was kept distinct from the Roman Army proper. At the time of the crucifixion they were called Pontius Pilate's Scots Guards, and their descendants were the nucleus of the First Royal Scots in later years.

Notes.—The oldest Regiment of Foot in the British Army. Traditionally regarded as the ancient body-guard of the Scottish kings, this famous corps was in the service of Sweden, as "Hepburn's Regiment," from 1625 to 1633; and in that of France from 1633 to 1678, when (under Dumbarton) it came to England. It received its title in 1684 in recognition of the capture of a Colour from the Moors at Tangier. At Sedgemoor (1685) it also captured the Duke of Monmouth's Standard.

17th.

1751-82, The 17th Regiment of Foot. Also "Forbes."

1881 (from) "The Leicestershire Regiment."

Nicknames—"The Bengal Tigers" (from its badge); "The Lily-whites" (from its facings).

Notes—Mainly raised near London; twelve regiments in all were formed in 1688, but this and the 16th (The Bedfordshire) are alone in commission now.

27th.

See above, Ticonderoga, 1758.

42nd.

See above, Ticonderoga, 1758.

55th.

See above, Ticonderoga, 1758.

77th.

1756-63, The 77th (Montgomery Highlanders) Regiment; disbanded 1763.

80th.

See above, Ticonderoga, 1758.

Royal Artillery.

See above, Ticonderoga, 1758.

I

PROVINCIAL REGIMENTS AT TICONDEROGA.

(The writer will have to admit that this list is more or less incomplete, even the N. Y. State Library at Albany had only scattered items. It would seem as if this would be a good subject for an article for some future meeting of the Association and any information will be gratefully received).

1758.

The New York Colonial Manuscripts, edited by Callaghan, page 732, in the list of regiments having officers wounded at the battle of July 8, 1758, gives the following regiments: Col. De-Lanceys, New York; Col. Babcock's, Rhode Island; Col. Fitche's, Connecticut; Col. Worcester's, Connecticut; Col. Bagley's, Massachusetts; Col. Partridge's, Massachusetts; Col. Preble's, Massachusetts; Col. Johnston's, New Jersey. Parkmen mentions Col. Brad-street with his regiment of boatmen, armed and drilled as soldiers and it is also certain that Roger's Rangers were with the expedition.

The year book of the Maine Chapter of the Society of Colonial Wars for 1900 gives much information in regard to Col. Preble's regiment, Maine being in 1758 a part of Massachusetts. Mention is made in this article of regiments officered by "Col. Doty, Col. Joseph Williams, Col. Nickols, Col. Whitings."

Also in the New York Colonial Manuscripts, Vol. 10, P. 827 it mentions a force of about 3,000 men nearly all of whom were provincials, under Col. Bradstreet, in the expedition against Fort Frontinac after the battle of July 8, 1758, and of the number of soldiers engaged, the list is given as New Yorkers 1112, Col.

Williams' regiment 413, Col. Douty's 248, Rhode Island 318, and Jersey 418."

It is not clear whether these regiments were at the battle of Ticonderoga and were not mentioned in list page 732 of the New York Colonial Manuscripts because none of the officers were wounded, or whether they were the same regiments but with different officers, a change having been made after the battle.

1759

The provincial regiments mentioned in Commissary Wilson's Orderly Book as being in the Ticonderoga expedition of 1759 are as follows: Col. Lyman's, Connecticut; Col. Whiting's, Connecticut; Col. Worcester's, Connecticut; Col. Fitch's, Connecticut; Col. Willard's, Massachusetts; Col. Ruggle's, Massachusetts; Col. Lovell's, New Hampshire; Col. Schuyler's, New Jersey; Col. Babcock's, Rhode Island.

J

BIOGRAPHICAL SKETCHES OF AS MANY OF THE OFFICERS OF 1758 AS COULD BE TRACED.

James Abercrombie.

James Abercrombie was promoted to a captaincy in the 42nd or 1st Battalion of the Royal Highlanders on the 16th of February, 1756. On the 5th of May, 1759, he was appointed aid de camp to Maj. Gen. Amherst, with whom he made the campaigns of that and the following year. On the 25th of July, 1760, he was appointed Major of the 78th or Fraser's Highlanders and in September following was employed by Gen. Amherst in communicating to the Marquis de Vaudreuil the conditions preparatory to the surrender of Montreal and in obtaining the signature of that governor to them. (Knox's Journal). The 78th having been disbanded in 1763, Major Abercrombie retired on half pay. On the 27th of March, 1770, he again entered active service as Lt. Colonel of the 22nd Regiment then serving in America under the command

New York Colonial Manuscripts by Broadhead, Weed, Parsons Co., Albany, 1856, page 160.

of Lt. Col. Gage and was killed in the memorable Battle of Bunker Hill on the 17th of June, 1775.

Hugh Arnot.

Hugh Arnot was taken from the half pay list and appointed a Lieutenant in the 42nd Highlanders, 9th April, 1756, at the augmentation of that Regiment on its coming to America, and was promoted to a Company on the 27th December, 1757. He served in the unfortunate affair of Ticonderoga in 1758, and in 1759 accompanied Amherst as above. On the 16th August, 1760, he exchanged into the 46th Foot, in which Regiment he continued to serve until 1769, when his name was dropped from the Army List.

Wilson's Orderly Book, p. 143.

Patrick Balneaves.

Patrick Balneaves, of Edradour, entered the 42nd, as Ensign, 28th January, 1756, and was promoted to be Lieutenant 1st April, 1758; he was wounded at Ticonderoga, 1758; and again at Martinico in 1762; became Captain-Lieutenant 23rd August, 1763, and left the army in 1770.

Stewart. Army Lists. N. Y. Colonial Manuscripts, p. 729, Vol. 10.

Allan Campbell.

Allan Campbell, son of Barcaldine, entered the Army as Ensign of the 43d (now the 42nd) Highlanders, Dec. 25, 1744, and served that year against the Pretender. Was made prisoner of war at Preston Pans, 21st Sept. 1745 and sent on parole to Perth. Was appointed lieutenant Dec. 1, 1746. He obtained a Company 13th of May, 1755, and the next year came to America, where he shared the difficulties and honors of the Regiment. In June, 1759, he was appointed Major for the campaign under Amherst, and was actively employed at the Head of the Grenadiers and Rangers, clearing the way for the army up the Lakes. He became major in the army 15th August, 1762, and went on halfpay on the reduction of the regiment in 1763, having obtained a grant of 5,000 acres of land at Crown Point. He served 19 years in the regiment. In 1770, he was appointed Major of the 36th or Herefordshire Foot, then

AT TICONDEROGA

Tablet on Boulder near French Lines at Fort Ticonderoga
Tablet in Black Watch Memorial at Ticonderoga

serving in Jamaica; became Lieutenant-Colonel in the army in May (1772), and of his regiment in January, 1778; Colonel in the Army, 17th Nov. 1780; Major-General in 1787; and died 1795. His Regiment did not serve in America during the Revolutionary War.

An extract from his will dated 2nd March 1787, reads: "And whereas I am under a grant from the Crown intitled to a considerable tract of land and heredits situate, lying and being in the Province of New York in the County of Albany in America, between Ticonderoga and Crown Point. * * I do hereby give, devise and bequeath unto my two sisters, Isabella Campbell, (wife of John C. of Archalader, in the Shire of Perth, in North Britain, aforesaid Esquire), and Jane Campbell of Edinchip, in the Shire of Perth, aforesaid, widow of Colin Campbell of Edinchip, aforesaid, Esq. deceased, their heirs, executors, Administraters, and Assigns, all my said track of land and heredits, in America," etc.

Browne, IV, 150.
Knox Journal, I, 373, 377, 387; II. 401.
Army List. Commissionary Wilson's Orderly Book. 1759. p. 18. Stewart of Garth Appendix.

Archibald Campbell.

Archibald Campbell. Born 1720. Eldest son of Duncan Campbell of Glendaruel and Lockhead. His mother was Elizabeth, daughter of the Rev. Archibald Campbell of Inverary. He was appointed Ensign 42d Regt. 23d Jan. 1756, Lieut. 28th July 1757, Captain 4th Dec. 1759. Died 3d June 1762.

Donald Campbell.

Donald Campbell, son of Donald Campbell Bailie of McKairn, Taynuilt Argyll, was appointed Ensign in the 42d Regt. of Foot, 5th May 1756. He was with one of the additional companies in the "Anandall" which sprang two leaks, lost her mizen mast, was attacked three times by Privateers (which they beat off with small arms), and was driven into the West Indies, so that she did not arrive in New York, in time for the company to join the attack on Ticonderoga. He was appointed Lieut. 24th July 1758 and retired 13th June 1761, having served with the Royal Highlanders from 1758 to 1761.

Highlanders in America by MacLean, page 176, N. Y. Colonial Documents, page 629.

Duncan Campbell (Killochronan, Island of Mall).

"Extract from the Memorial of Captain Duncan Campbell, American Loyalist Claims.

"Humbly Sheweth, that he was a native of Great Britain and he was appointed Ensign in the 42nd Highlanders 26 January 1756, in which Corps he served the war before last in America and the West Indies. And in August 1763 the Regiment was ordered on an expedition to the relief of Fort Pitt, then invested by the savages.

On the march he was severely wounded at the battle of Bushy Run, and for a long time rendered unfit for service. (In this skirmishing warfare the troops suffered much from the want of water and the extreme heat of the weather) which occasioned his retiring on half pay in 1764.

He soon thereafter settled at Fredricksburg, Dutchess Co. in the Prov. of New York (in 1769) and purchased a valuable track of land from Colonel Beverly Robinson and others on good terms. In 1775 he was Colonel of Militia and Magistrate for the said county.

That at the commencement of the troubles he took an early and decided part in favor of His Majesty's government, which rendered him so obnoxious to the popular party where he dwelt that he was obliged to fly to New York, to save his life, from the family and abandon his property in June 1775. That soon after his arrival there he engaged as an officer in the 2nd Battalion Highland Emigrant's in which he continued doing duty until the cessation of hostilities, and consequent reduction of the Regiment in Nova Scotia, in which Province he now dwells. (2 Jannary 1784).

That early in June 1775 he got on board the Asia ship of war (64 gun frigate) then stationed in New York and soon after was joined by some recruits he had engaged to follow him. In July thereafter he went to Boston where Gen. Gage then Commander-in-Chief, gave him command of an armed transport in which he returned to New York where he enlisted and received on board about 60 more recruits. That in September he returned again to Boston where he left all his recruits except 26 which were left on board as Marines, on the 8 October he was sent back on the same service. But on the 16 of the same month was unfortunately shipwrecked on the coast of New Jersey.

On this service he lost all his money and baggage to the amount of £100. This loss His Excellency Sir William Howe, then Commander-in-Chief, would not think of reimbursing at the time.

AT FORT TICONDEROGA

Officers Quarters or West Barracks
Two views from same point showing before and
after restoration

The Block House, summer residence of Howland Pell
A reproduction of the Germain redoubt
The Pavilion, summer residence of S. H. Pell. Built

In consequence of the shipwreck he and his party had the misfortune to be made prisoners and was carried to Philadelphia where he was fourteen months in a small apartment of the dismal goal where he contracted a sickness which was likely to prove fatal to him.

How soon he was taken his family were turned out of doors and deprived of everything they had except some wearing apparell. The distressed situation of the family so driven from their home may be easier felt than described. It brought on for a beginning the untimely death of an amiable wife, and deprived his five infant children of a mother's care whereby they for some time became objects of compassion which he was unable to rescue them from. Until he was exchanged and joined his Regiment (in January 1777) he thereafter continued to serve during the war.

N. B. The Memorialist was appointed Second Oldest Captain in the 2nd Batt. 84th Regiment the 14 June 1775 and was reduced in October 1783 without a step of preferment in the Regt. or in the Line.

Captain 4th Breadalbane Regt. of Fencibles 2nd Batt. 1 March 1793; Major 17 Feb. 1794; Lieut. Col. 9 Dec. 1795; Regiment disbanded 18 April 1799. He died at Edinburgh in Dec. 1799.

Major Sir Duncan Campbell of Barcaldine, Bart. C. V. O.
Stewart, I 279; II, Appendix No. 11.

John Campbell of Duneavis.

John Campbell, of Duneaves, Perthshire, was originally a private in the Black Watch. In 1743, he was presented, with Gregor McGregor, to George II, as a specimen of the Highland soldier and performed at St. James the broadsword exercise and that of the Lochaber axe, before his Majesty and a number of General officers. Each got a gratuity of a guinea, which they gave to the porter at the gate of the palace as they passed out. Mr. Campbell obtained an Ensigncy in 1745 for his bravery at the battle of Fontenoy; was promoted to be Captain-Lieutenant, 16th February, 1756, and landed in New York the following June. He was among the few resolute men who forced their way into the work at Ticonderoga, on the 8th of July, where he was killed.

John Campbell of Glendaruel.

John Campbell of Glendaruel, born in 1721, was appointed Ensign of the 42nd Regt. of Foot 25th Sept., 1745; Lieutenant 16th

May, 1748; Captain Lieut. 2nd July 1759; and Captain 20th July 1760; Captain 27th or Inniskilling Regiment of Foot 25th March 1762; Major Supt. of Indian Affairs in the Province of Quebec 2nd July, 1773; Lieut. Col. of Indian Affairs 29th August 1777; and Colonel 16th Nov. 1790.

He married Marianna St. Lucan (date not given) and died Montreal, 23rd June 1795.

"In the course of a long and meritorious service with his Regiment, the 42nd Highlanders, in all its campaigns from the Rebellion in 1745 to the attack on Ticonderoga, where he was wounded on the 8th July, 1758, and the conquest of Canada, Martinique, and Havanna. He subsequently served in the expedition commanded by General Burgoyne, at the head of a number of Indians, and was distinguished for his spirited conduct as an officer, adorned by that elegance and politeness which mark the accomplished gentleman and his virtues in private life endeared him to his family and companions.

His remains were attended to the grave in a manner suitable to his rank. Not only by a very numerous assembly of citizens of all ranks, but by a large body of Indian warriors, whose very decent behavior evinced the sincerity with which they partook of the universal regret occasioned by the loss of so very respectable a member of society."

Major Sir Duncan Campbell of Barcaldine, Bart. C. V. O.

John Campbell of Strachur.

John Campbell of Strachur, in the Highlands of Scotland, entered the Army in June, 1745, as Lieutenant of Loudon's Highlanders; served through the Scotch Rebellion; made the Campaign in Flanders, 1747, and was promoted to a company on the 1st October of that year. At the peace of 1748, he went on Half-Pay and so remained until the 9th April, 1756, when he was appointed to the 42nd Highlanders previous to the embarcation of that Regiment for America. He was wounded in the attack on Ticonderoga in 1758, and was appointed by General Amherst Major of the 17th Foot on the 11th July, 1759; was promoted to be Lieutenant-

Colonel in the Army, 1st February, 1762 and commanded his Regiment in the expedition that year against Martinico and Havana. On the 1st May, 1773, he became Lieutenant-Colonel of the 57th or West Middlesex Foot, returned to America in 1776 with his Regiment at the breaking out of the Revolution; was appointed Maj. General 19th February, 1779, Colonel of his Regiment 2d November, 1780, and commanded the British Forces in West Florida, where after a gallant though ineffectual defence he was obliged to surrender Pensacola to the Spaniards 10th May, 1781. He became Lieutenant-General 28th September, 1787; General in the Army, 26th January, 1797, and died in the fore part of 1806.

Brown, IV., 155, 159.
Stewart's Sketches of the Highlanders, I, 295, 306, 359, 370; II. 5, app. iii; Knox Journal, I, 373; II, 401; Beatson's Naval and Mil. Mem. V, 50, 226-233; VI, 274-280; Army Lists. Wilson's Orderly Book, page 94.

Moses Campbell.

A native of Scotland, joined the 42nd Regt. and was promoted Sergeant.

Served with this Regiment throughout the war of French and Indians in America of 1756-63, discharged at the reduction, and settled with his family on a portion of Maj. Allan Campbell's (same Regt.) grant of land, situated on the south (bank) side of Lake Champlain, between Crown Point (about 5 miles above the point) and Ticonderoga.

Also served (possibly in the Royal Highland Emigrants, bounty 50s rendezvous Lake Champlain, 1775) in the War of Independence of 1775, (for which his property was confiscated, including boats.)

He died in active (British) service on the 18th Feb. 1781.

His widow, Elizabeth, and seven children claimed 366 pounds for losses, allowed 80 pounds.

N. B. On behalf of her son, Alexander, (aged 21 years), 50 pounds, who complained that one of the rebels was now living in his house, Feb. 1783.

Gordon Graham.

Gordon Graham of Drainie in the Highlands of Scotland, was appointed ensign in the 43rd Highlanders in Oct. 25, 1739, and was made lieutenant June 24, 1743. He served in Flanders and shared in the defeat at Fontenoy in 1745, after which the Regiment returned home. In 1747 he made another campaign in Flanders. On August 7, 1747, he was appointed captain. In 1749 the number of the regiment was changed to the 42d and Mr. Graham obtained a company in it 3d June, 1752, came to America in 1756, was at the surrender of Fort William Henry under Colonel Munro in 1757, and was wounded at Ticonderoga in 1758. The Major of the Regiment having been killed on that occasion Captain Graham succeeded to the vacancy, July 17th, 1758, and made the campaign of 1759 and 1760 under Amherst. He next served in the West Indies in the expedition against Martinique and July 9, 1762, became Lieutenant Colonel of the Regiment, which returned to New York, and in the year 1763, proceeded to the relief of Fort Pitt, defeating the Indians on the way in the Battle of Bushy Run. In December, 1770, he retired after 31 years of service in the Regiment. As his name does not appear in the army list of 1771 it is presumed that he died at this time.

Brown's Highland Clans IV, 139, 159. Beatson's Naval and Mil. Mem. II, 530. Wilson's Orderly Book, p. 14.

John Graham.

John Graham was the brother of Thomas; entered the 42nd regiment as Ensign and was promoted to a Lieutenancy 25th January, 1776; was wounded at Ticonderoga 1758; became Captain in February, 1762, and was again wounded at Bushy Run in 1763; shortly after which his company having been disbanded, he went on half pay. He rejoined the regiment 25th December, 1765, and is dropped in 1772, having attained the rank of field officer.

Stewart I, 359, Army Lists. N. Y. Col. Manuscripts, p. 729, Vol. 10.

Thomas Graham.

Thomas Graham, or Graeme, of Duchay, entered the 43rd, or Black Watch, as Ensign June 30, 1741; was promoted to a Lieutenancy August 6, 1746, and obtained a company February 15, 1756, shortly before the regiment, then the 42nd, came to America. He served in the several Campaigns on the northern lakes; was

Grave of Jane McCrea, Union Cemetery, between Hudson Falls and Fort Edward. Major Duncan Campbell is now buried in this lot.

wounded at Ticonderoga in 1758; was again wounded at the battle of Bushy Run, near Pittsburg, in 1763; served in the subsequent campaigns against the Indians, and embarked for Ireland in 1767. He succeeded Major Reid 31st March, 1770, and became Lieutenant-Colonel 12th December following. He retired from the army December, 1771, after 30 years of service.

Army Lists. Stewart. N. Y. Colonial Manuscripts, p. 729, Vol. 10.

Francis Grant.

Francis Grant, son of the Laird of Grant, and brother of Sir Ludovick Grant, of Grant, Scotland, was received from half-pay in Loudon's Regiment and was made ensign in the Black Watch Oct. 25, 1739. Nov. 5, 1739, he was made lieutenant; June 18, 1743, captain; and Oct. 3, 1745, he became major. A vacancy occurring in the lieutenant-colonelcy, in December, 1755, the men of the Regiment subscribed a sum of money among themselves to purchase the step for him, but it was not required; he had already obtained his promotion. He accompanied the Regiment to America in 1756 and was present at the bloody battle of Ticonderoga, July 8, 1758, where he was wounded. In the following year he accompanied Amherst on his expedition, and in 1760 was in command of the van of the Army from Oswego to Montreal. In 1761 he commanded the Army sent to the south to chastise the Cherokees. He served as Brigadier-General in the expedition against Martinico in 1762, and on the 19th of February of that year became colonel in the army. On July 9, 1762, after twenty-three years of service in the Black Watch Regiment, he was removed and appointed to the command of the 90th Light Infantry. In August, 1762, he commanded the 4th Brigade at the siege of Havana and went on half pay at the peace of 1763. In November, 1768, he became colonel of the 63rd; Major-General in 1770; and Lieutenant-General in 1777. He died at the beginning of 1782 (Army Lists).

Lieut.-Gen. Grant's daughter was married to the Hon. and Rt. Rev. George Murray, fourth son of the Duke of Athol, and Bishop of St. David's.

Brown's Highland Clans, IV, 155.
Knox's Journal, II, 404, 410, 465.
Beatson N. and M., Mem. III, 363, 359.
Debrett's Peerage. Wilson's Orderly Book, p. 3.

James Grant.

James Grant, appointed Ensign, Nov. 20, 1746; Lieutenant, Jan. 22, 1756; Captain, Dec. 26, 1760; removed Aug. 13, 1762, after 16 years of service in the Regiment and was made Fort-Major Limerick. Died in 1778. He was wounded at Ticonderoga.

Stewart of Garth, Appendix.

William Grant.

William Grant, appointed Ensign, Oct. 1, 1745; Lieutenant, May 22, 1746; Captain, July 23, 1758; Major, Dec. 5, 1777; retired August, 1778, after 33 years of service with rank of Brevet Lieut-Colonel. He was wounded at the battle of Ticonderoga.

Stewart of Garth, Appendix.

James Gray.

James Gray was taken from the Half-pay list and appointed Lieutenant in the 42nd Royal Highlanders 30th January, 1756. His name is omitted in the Army List of 1765.

Stewart's Highlanders. Wilson's Orderly Book, page 83.

Robert Gray.

Robert Gray, appointed Ensign, June 6, 1745; Lieutenant, June 9, 1747; Captain, July 22, 1758. He was wounded at Ticonderoga. Aug. 2, 1759, after 14 years of service in the Regiment, he was promoted to the 55th Regiment. He died in 1771 with rank of Lieut.-Colonel.

Stewart of Garth, Appendix.

Alexander McIntosh.

Alexander McIntosh was taken from half pay in 1756 and appointed Lieutenant in the 42nd. He was wounded at Ticonderoga, 1758, and again at Martinico in 1762, and was promoted to a company 24th July of the same year. He went on half pay in 1763 and was not again called on active service until 25th December,

1770, when he was appointed to the 10th regiment then serving in America. Captain McIntosh was killed at the storming of Fort Washington, 16th November, 1776.

Army Lists. Beatson's Naval and Military Memoirs. N. Y. Colonial Manuscripts, p. 729, Vol. 10.

Norman McLeod.

Norman McLeod entered the army as ensign of the 42d January 1756, and was promoted to Lieutenancy in the 69th in June 1761. At the peace of 1763 he elected to remain in this country and received 3,000 acres of land and retired on half pay. Sometime later he was appointed Commissioner at Niagara under Sir William Johnson. At the breaking out of the War of the Revolution he offered his services to Governor Martin of North Carolina. Later he was captured and was a prisoner for about five years.

Wm. M. McBean, Secy. St. Andrew's Society of the State of New York.

John MacNeil.

John MacNeil was appointed ensign, Aug. 6, 1742, lieutenant Oct. 10, 1745; Captain, Dec. 16, 1752; Major, July 9, 1762. He died at the siege of Havana in 1762 after 20 years of service in the Regiment.

Stewart of Garth, Appendix.

David Milne.

David Mill, or Milne, received a commission as Lieutenant in this Corps 19th July, 1757; was wounded at Ticonderoga in 1758, and again at Martinique in 1762; retired from the army at the peace of 1763.

N. Y. Colonial Manuscripts, p. 729, Vol. 10.

James Murray.

James Murray, second son of Lord George Murray, by his marriage with Amelia Murray, heiress of Strowan and Glencarse, and grandson of the first Duke of Atholl, was born at Tullibardine on the 19th of March, 1734, and it is interesting to know that Lord John Murray, who was destined in after years to be his colonel, was called upon to be his godfather. A commission as Lieutenant in the Saxon Grenadier Guards was obtained for him in 1749, and he joined his regiment in 1751. He served against the forces of Frederick the Great until the Saxon Army capitulated at Pirna on the Elbe in October, 1756. He was released on parole and returned to Scotland in 1757 and on the nomination of his uncle, James Duke of Atholl, was given a captain's commission in the Black Watch and was placed in command of one of the three additional companies then being raised for service in America. He reached New York in April, 1758, and commanded Captain Reid's company in the unsuccessful attack on Ticonderoga—his own company having been left in garrison at Fort Edward. He was wounded but was soon able to return to duty and took part in the successful expedition of 1759 to Lake Champlain. Toward the close of that year he was given command—by Lord John Murray's desire—of the Grenadier Company of the newly-raised 2nd Battalion, and with this battalion he served in the advance on Montreal in 1760 and in the capture of Martinique in 1762. He was wounded here and invalided home and was on sick leave for more than six years.* He rejoined the Black Watch in 1768 and in 1769 was appointed Captain-lieutenant in the 3rd Foot Guards, obtaining his promotion as Captain and Lieutenant-colonel the following year. In 1772 he was elected member of Parliament for Perthshire, a position which he held for twenty-two years. He was appointed Governor of Upnor Castle in 1775 and Fort William in 1780, but these were merely nominal posts and did not interfere with his other duties. In 1776 he bought Strowan (originally the property of his mother), from his nephew, the fourth Duke of Atholl.

On the outbreak of the War of Independence, Col. Murray offered to raise a regiment of Highlanders for service in America, but this offer was refused, and in March, 1777, he was sent out to join the brigade of Guards under General Howe in New Jersey. He was with Lord Cornwallis at Quibbletown and presumably took part in the actions at Brandywine and Germantown in 1777. He spent the following winter in quarters at Philadelphia, and left America in the summer of 1778 and joined the Atholl Highlanders in Ireland in September of that year, of which regiment he was given the command. This regiment remained in Ireland during the war, at the conclusion of which it was disbanded. James Murray was appointed Lieutenant-colonel-commandant of the 78th Highlanders in 1783, but as he was already a general officer he never did any duty with this regiment. After 1783 General Murray resided a good deal at Strowan; in 1786 he was promoted full Colonel of the 78th (by that time the 72nd), and in 1793 he was made Lieutenant-general. In March, 1794, he felt himself obliged to resign his seat in Parliament owing to ill health and a few days later—on the 19th of March—he died in London and was buried in St. Margaret's, Westminster.

Of Lord George Murray's three sons, General James seems to have been the one who most resembled his father. He had inherited the Jacobite General's sympathetic knowledge of Highland character, something of his pride, and the same affectionate disposition. And that he had at least a share of his father's determination. and presence of mind is shown by two anecdotes which have been handed down with regard to him. One of these refers to his earlier days, and is to the effect that, having been attacked by a highwayman one night that he was driving over a heath near London, he leant out of the window of the chaise, "groped in the dark for the ears of his assailant's horse," and with the brief but expressive exclamation. "Thereut's-" fired a shot which ended the highwayman's career. The other relates that during the Gordon Riots of 1780 Colonel James Murray was seated next Lord George Gordon in the House of Commons at the very moment at which the mob threatened to break into the House. Colonel Murray with a soldier's instinct drew his sword, pointed it at Lord George, and notwithstanding that he was his cousin, declared his intention of

---

Army Lists: Brown's Highl. Clans, IV, 159, 300, 304, 306. Wilson's Orderly Book, p. 67. Military History of Perthshire, p. 411-413.

Stewart of Garth gives the following in regard to General Murray's wound, received at the capture of Martinique; (page 126, Vol. 10.)
"The musket ball entered his left side, under the lower rib, passed up through the left lobe of the lung, (as ascertained after his death) crossed his chest, and mounting up to his right shoulder, lodged under the scapula. His case being considered desperate, the only object of the surgeon was to make his situation as easy as possible for, the few hours they supposed he had to live; but, to the great surprise of all, he was on his legs in a few weeks, and, before he reached England, was quite recovered, or at least his health and appetite were restored. He was never afterwards, however, able to lie down; and during the thirty-two years of his subsequent life, he slept in an upright posture, supported in his bed by pillows.

running him through the body if a single one of the rioters should enter. His promptness saved the situation, but he had committed a breach of the privileges of the House and was ordered to apologize on bended knee to the Speaker. Colonel Murray made the required amende, but on rising from his knee took out his handkerchief and dusted it, remarking, "Damned Dirty House this; sooner it's cleaned out the better."

Lord John Murray.

Lord John Murray, born on the 14th of April, 1711, was the eldest son of John, first Duke of Atholl, by his second wife, the Hon. Mary Ross, and half-brother to John, Marquess of Tullibardine, and Lord George Murray. He became an ensign in the 3rd Foot Guards (now the Scots Guards) in 1727, and a captain in the same regiment in 1738. Immediately after the mutiny of the regiment in 1743 he applied for the colonelcy in the 42nd or Black Watch, but he did not obtain the appointment he so greatly desired until two years later. In July, 1743, he was appointed first aide-de-camp to George II and was in attendance on the King in Germany at the close of the Dettingen campaign, but returned to England without having taken part in any engagements. In April 1745, when at last gazetted colonel of the Black Watch, he proceeded to join his regiment in Flanders, but arrived too late for Fontenoy. He distinguished himself, however, during the subsequent retreat of the British army to Brussels, by his defence of a pass which the French attacked by night. For this service he was publicly thanked by the Duke of Cumberland. In 1745 he returned home with his regiment but in 1747 he was in the Netherlands taking part in the attempted relief of Hulst. After the surrender of the town by the Dutch Governor, Lord John commanded the rearguard in the retreat to Welsharden, and shortly afterwards, having been ordered to take part in the defence of Bergen-op-Zoom, he was placed in command of the British troops in the lines there. At the close of operations he received a message of approbation from the King.

In 1755 he was promoted major-general, and in 1758 lieutenant-general, but although he offered his services more than once, he was not employed abroad during the Seven Years' War. He took the keenest interest, however, in all the exploits of his regiment

From "A Military History of Perthshire"

Lord John Murray, Colonel the Black Watch, 1745 to 1787

and worked hard to raise a second battalion in 1758. Stewart of Garth tells us that when the men who had been disabled at Ticonderoga appeared before the Board of Chelsea to claim their pensions, Lord John went with them and explained their case in such a manner to the commissioners that they were all successful. He gave them money, got them a free passage to Perth, and offered a house and garden to all who chose to settle on his estate. General Stewart also describes how, when the 42nd at last returned from America in 1767, Lord John, who had been for weeks at Cork awaiting its arrival, marched into that town at its head.

Lord John was a great deal with the regiment while it was quartered in Ireland, and, according to Stewart of Garth, was "ever attentive to the interest of the officers and vigilant that their promotion should not be interrupted by ministerial or other influence." He was also "unremitting in his exertions to procure the appointment of good officers, and of officers who understood perfectly the peculiar dispositions and character of the men." For this reason he strenuously endeavored to exclude all but the members of Scots—and more especially Highland—families. He was equally particular that only Gaelic-speaking men and Protestants should be recruited for the ranks.

In spite of his military duties Lord John resided a good deal in the country—and not only at the home of his boyhood—for early in life he bought Pitnacree in Strathtay, and in later years he had also a house in Perth. He represented Perthshire in Parliament from 1734 to 1761. In 1758 he married Miss Dalton of Bannercross—a Derbyshire heiress, by whom he had one daughter. In 1770 he became a full general. His last military achievement was the raising in 1779 and 1780 (at his own expense) of another second battalion to the 42nd. This battalion so distinguished itself in India that in 1786 it was placed permanently on the establishment under the title of the 73rd Regiment. The veteran to whose patriotism it owed its existence died on the 26th day of May, 1787, at the age of seventy-six, the senior officer in the Army.

Lord John made the most of such chances as occurred of distinguishing himself in the field, but those opportunities were small for he never served in any war but the Austrian Succession.

It is therefore as the Colonel of the Black Watch that his name has survived—as a man who understood the Highland soldiers well enough to wish to command them at a time when to many that might have seemed a task of great difficulty—and who, having at last obtained the post he desired, completely identified himself with the interests of his men, and for upwards of half a century was the "friend and supporter of every deserving officer and soldier in the regiment."

Military History of Perthshire, page 382-384.

John Reid.

John Reid was the eldest son of Alexander Robertson of Straloch, but the head of the family had always been known as "Baron Reid" and the General and his younger brother, Alexander (who was an officer in the 42nd), adopted the more distinctive surname early in life. He was born at Inverchroskie in Strathardle, on the 13th of February, 1721, and received his early education at Perth. Being destined for the law, he was afterwards sent to Edinburgh University. Nature, however, had intended him for a soldier, and in June, 1745, having recruited the necessary quota of men, he obtained a commission as lieutenant in Loudon's Highlanders. He was taken prisoner at Prestonpans the following September, but when released the following spring he rejoined his regiment and was able to render important service to the Government. From 1747 to 1748 he served in Flanders with Loudon's Highlanders and took part in the defence of Bergen-op-Zoom, but on the reduction of his regiment at the Peace of Aix-la-Chapelle he was placed on half-pay. In 1751 he bought a captain-lieutenant's commission in the Black Watch and in 1752 a commission as captain in the same regiment. Four years later on the outbreak of the war with France, he sailed with his regiment to America. He was not present at the first attack on Ticonderoga as he had been left behind sick at Albany, and his company was commanded in that desperate engagement by Captain James Murray. In 1759, Reid, by that time a major, took part in the second advance to Lake Champlain, which resulted in the surrender of Forts Ticonderoga and Crown Point; and on him devolved the command of the 42nd during the greater part of the campaign of 1760 which ended with the capture of Montreal and the expulsion of the French from Canada.

Reid remained in America with the 42nd until Dec., 1761, when he accompanied it to the West Indies. He served in the capture of Martinique and at the storming of Morne Tortenson, on Jan. 24, 1762, was in command of the 1st Battalion of his regiment. His battalion suffered heavy loss and he was wounded in two places, but recovered in time to take part in the expedition against Havana of that same year. After the surrender of Cuba he returned to America. In 1764 Reid acted as second-in-command of Colonel Bouquet's arduous but successful expedition against the Indians on the Ohio and Muskingum Rivers. In the following year we hear of him fitting out an expedition which was to be sent to the Illinois country under the command of Captain Thomas Stirling of the 42nd.

About 1760, Reid married an American lady of Scots descent, Susanna Alexander, daughter of James Alexander, surveyor-general of New York and New Jersey. She owned property on Otter Creek in what is now the State of Vermont, which was added to and improved by her husband with the result that at the end of ten years Reid owned "about thirty-five thousand acres of very valuable land" near Crown Point and had "obtained from the Governor and Council of New York a warrant of survey for fifteen thousand more," which he intended to "erect" into a manor.

In 1767 the Royal Highland Regiment left America for Ireland and Reid presumably accompanied it. In 1770 Reid retired on half-pay, intending no doubt to settle down to the enjoyment and improvement of his American estates. However, in 1772 his tenants were expelled by the people of Bennington "on the pretence of having claim to that country under the Government of New Hampshire, notwithstanding that the King in Council had, ten years before, decreed Connecticut River to be the Eastern Boundary of New York." In 1775 war broke out with the American colonists, and though his case finally came before the Commissioners for American Claims, the only compensation awarded him was a trifling allowance for mills he had erected and for fees he had paid for surveys. In May, 1778 his father's estate, Straloch, passed under the hammer as he was unable to pay the mortgages and his son could give him no help.

Notwithstanding that he was a comparatively poor man, in 1779-1780 Reid raised at his own expense a regiment of foot, of which he was appointed colonel. This was called the 95th and was disbanded in 1783. In 1781 Reid was promoted major-general, and in 1793 a lieutenant-general. He was appointed colonel of the 88th Regiment (Connaught Rangers) in November, 1794, and became a general in 1798. In 1803, when an invasion was hourly expected, Reid, in response to an order that all general officers not employed on the staff should transmit their addresses to the Adjutant-General, wrote that though in the eighty-second years of his age "and very deaf and infirm," he was still ready to use his feeble arm in defence of his country. He died in the Haymarket on the 6th of February, 1807, and was buried in St. Margaret's, Westminster.

The General would probably have had but little property to dispose of at his death, had he not in 1796 succeeded to a valuable estate of some four or five thousand acres in Nova Scotia, which was left to him by his cousin, Gen. John Small, "as a mark of . . . . respect . . . . and attachment to the preservation of his name and representation for succeeding ages." Reid's daughter had made a marriage of which he disapproved, she had no children, and his only brother had died in 1762 during the siege of Havana. It was probably these circumstances that induced him to realize the property in Nova Scotia and at the time of his death he was worth some £52,000. This entire fortune, went after the death of his daughter, to the University of Edinburgh to found a musical professorship. He also left directions that a concert should be given annually on or about his birthday to commence with several pieces of his own composition, among the first of which is that of the "Garb of Old Gaul," a composition written by Sir Charles Erskine, but set to music by Reid while major of the 42nd, and which has ever sence been a regimental march.

Reid also composed several military marches and was esteemed the best gentleman player on the German flute in England. It may

MAJOR-GENERAL JOHN SMALL

*(From a Medallion in the possession of
Mrs. Small of Dirnanean)*

GENERAL SIR THOMAS STIRLING
OF ARDOCH AND STROWAN,
BART.

*(From a Miniature in the possession of
Captain Graham Stirling of Strowan)*

GENERAL JOHN REID

(From a Portrait in the Music Class-room of Edinburgh University)

From "A Military History of Perthshire"

Officers in the Black Watch 1758-9

safely be predicted that as long as the University exists this old Perthshire soldier of the 18th century will be remembered as one of its benefactors.

John Small.

John Small was the third son of Patrick Small, who married Magdalen Robertson, sister of Alexander Robertson, the father of General John Reid. Reid and Small were thus not only neighbors and brother-officers, but first cousins, and were evidently on terms of close friendship. Born in Strathardle, Atholl, Scotland, in 1730, Small, like many of his countrymen of that date, began his military career with the Scots Brigade in Holland, being appointed a 2nd lieutenant in the Earl of Drumlanrig's Regiment when it was raised for service of the States-General in 1747. How long he remained abroad is unknown but it is probable that he returned to England when the regiment was reduced in 1752. He did not, however, obtain a commission in the British army until four years later, when he was appointed lieutenant in the 42nd, just prior to its departure for America. So far as is known, Small took part in all the campaigns in which his regiment was engaged from 1756 to 1763. He fought at Ticonderoga in 1758, served with General Amherst's successful expedition to Lake Champlain in the following year, and took part in the operations which completed the conquest of Canada in 1760. After the surrender of Montreal he was sent in charge of French prisoners to New York, and we learn from a brother officer that General Amherst had great confidence in him, and frequently employed him "on particular services." Two years later he served in the capture of Martinique and Havana and obtained his promotion as captain.

At the peace of 1763 Small was placed on half-pay, but, according to General Stewart, he was almost immediately put on the full-pay list of the North British Fusiliers (21st) and when in 1767 the Black Watch left for Europe, most of the men of that regiment who had volunteered to stay in America joined the Fusiliers in order to serve under Small, who was "deservedly popular" with them. Small, however, cannot have served long with the 21st, for in the same year in which the Black Watch left America he was appointed "major of brigade" to the forces in North America.

It was probably during the interval between the Seven Years' War and the war with the Americans that he began to acquire the property in Nova Scotia, part of which he afterwards bequeathed to his cousin, John Reid. We have some indication that during this period he interested himself in local politics and formed the friendship of at least one American which was of value to him later.

Small served throughout the War of Independence though but rare glimpses are obtained of him. He was present as a brigade-major at the battle of Bunker Hill, June 17, 1777, and in the course of that day his life was saved by the American General Putnam, who, seeing Small standing alone at a time when all around him had fallen, struck up the barrels of his men's muskets to save his life. Shortly after this, Small raised the 2nd battalion of the Royal Highland Regiment and was appointed major-commandant. In 1778 the regiment was numbered the 84th and in 1780 he was promoted to lieutenant-colonel-commandant of his battalion. He is said to have joined Sir Henry Clinton at New York in 1779, but it is more probable that he was stationed for the most part in Nova Scotia. In March, 1783, Small and his battalion were at Fort Edward, New York, and in the following autumn the battalion was disbanded at Windsor, Nova Scotia, where many of the men settled and formed the present town of Douglas.

Small, once more on half-pay, returned home and in 1790 was promoted colonel and three years later was appointed lieutenant governor of Guernsey. In October, 1794, he became major-general and on the 17th of March, 1796, he died in Guernsey and was buried in the church of St. Peter Port.

General Stewart of Garth wrote of General John Small that "No chief of former days ever more fairly secured the attachment of his clan, and no chief, certainly, ever deserved it better. With an enthusiastic and almost romantic love for his country and coun-trymen, it seemed as if the principal object of his life had been to serve them, and promote prosperity. Equally brave in leading them in the field, and kind, just, and conciliating in quarters, they would have indeed been ungrateful if they regarded him otherwise

---

Stewart II, 143. Military Hist., of Perthshire, pp. 396-399.

than as they did. There was not an instance of desertion in his battalion."

James Stewart of Urrard.

James Stewart of Urrard, obtained a company in the 42nd, July 18th, 1757. He was wounded at Ticonderoga, 1758. He sold out after the peace.

Stewart I, 306, 359. N. Y. Col. MSS., p. 729, Vol. 10.

Thomas Stirling.

Thomas Stirling, second son of Sir Henry Stirling, of Ardoch, was born October 8, 1731. He began his military career in the Dutch service, being given a commission as ensign in the 1st Battalion of Col. Marjoribanks' Regiment on the 30th of September, 1747, and was probably placed on half-pay when the establishment of the Scots Brigade was reduced in 1752. On the 24th of July, 1757, having been nominated by James, Duke of Atholl, and having raised the requisite number of men, he was gazetted captain of one of the three companies added to the 42nd in that year. In November, 1757, he sailed for America, where he served with his regiment in the campaigns of the ensuing years, though he was not present at the first attack on Ticonderoga, owing to the fact that the new companies had been left behind to garrison Fort Edward. He took part in the capture of Martinique in 1762 and was wounded but was able to serve in the capture of Havana later in that year. He returned with his regiment to America and in August, 1765, was sent in command of a company to take possession of Fort de Chartes on the Mississippi. After holding this fort that winter and spring, he returned with his detachment to the regiment in June, 1766. The following year the 42nd left America and for upwards of eight years was quartered in Ireland, after which it was for a short time in Scotland. In 1770 Stirling was gazetted major of the regiment, and 1771 lieutenant-Colonel-commandant. Hostilities broke out with the Americans in 1775, and, Stirling, having in five months raised the strength of his regiment from 350 men to 1,200, returned with it in the following spring to America, where he commanded it continuously for three years during the war. He took part in the engagement at Brooklyn, the attack on Fort

Washington, the expedition to Pennsylvania, battle of Monmouth, and others. During 1778-9 he was stationed at or near New York. In June, 1779, he accompanied a force under General Mathews through New Jersey in an attempt to rally the supposed loyalists of that state. This was unsuccessful and ended in the destruction of the town of Springfield. General Stirling was so severely wounded while leading the attack that he could take no further part in the war. His thigh was broken and fearing to be rendered incapable of further service he refused to have it amputated. He recovered and was invalided home but he does not appear after this to have been ever again fit for active duty. In 1782 he was promoted major-general and appointed colonel of the 71st Foot, but his regiment was disbanded the following year. His services were rewarded with a baronetcy and in 1790, he became colonel of the 41st Regiment. In 1796 he was promoted lieutenant-general, and in 1799 he succeeded his brother in the baronetcy of Ardock. He attained the rank of general in 1801 and died unmarried on the 9th of May, 1808.

Kenneth Tolmie.

Kenneth Tolmie was commissioned a lieutenant in the 42nd Highlanders, 23rd January, 1756, and promoted to the Command of a Company 27th July, 1760. His name is dropped after the Peace of 1763.

Wilson's Orderly Book, p. 166.

Alexander Turnbull.

Alexander Turnbull of Stracathro, appointed ensign, June 3, 1752; lieutenant, Sept. 27, 1756; captain, Aug. 14, 1762. After 11 years of service, he went on half-pay in 1763; full pay of the 32nd Foot. He died in 1804 with rank of major.

Stewart of Garth, Appendix.

K

ORIGINAL REGIMENTAL LIST OF THE BLACK WATCH.

*From A Military History of Perthshire, pages 51, 52, and
The Black Watch Chronicle, 1913, pages 6-8.*

No. 1 Company.

Colonel and Captain John, Earl of Crawford. Died 1748.
Captain-Lieutenant Duncan Mackfarland. Retired 1744.
Ensign Gilbert Stewart of Kincraigie.

No. 2 Company.

Lieutenant-Colonel and Captain Sir Robert Munro, Bart., of Foulis.
   Killed at Falkirk 1746.
Lieutenant Paul Macferson.
Ensign Archibald Macknab, younger son of the Laird of Macnab.
   Died Lieut. General, 1790.

No. 3 Company.

Major and Captain George Grant. Removed from the service by
   sentence of Court-martial, 1746.
Lieutenant John MacKenzie of Rencraig (?Kincraig).
Ensign Collin Campbell.

No. 4 Company.

Captain Collin Campbell, Jr., of Monzie. Retired 1743.
Lieutenant Alexander Macdonald
Ensign James Campbell of Glenfalloch. Died of wounds at Fon-
   tenoy.

No. 5 Company.

Captain James Colquhoun of Luss. Promoted to be Major. Re-
   tired in 1748.
Lieutenant George Ramsay.
Ensign James Campbell of Stronslanie.[1]

No. 6 Company.

Captain John Campbell of Carrick. Killed at Fontenoy.
Lieutenant John MacLean of Kingairloch.
Ensign Dougall Stewart (of Appin?).

No. 7 Company.

Captain Collin Campbell of Balliemore. Retired.
Lieutenant Malcom Frazer, son of Culduthel.[2] Killed at Bergen-op-Zoom, 1747.
Ensign Dougal Stewart.

No. 8 Company.

Captain George Munro of Culcairn, brother of Foulis. Killed 1746.
Lieutenant Lewis Grant of Auchterblair.
Ensign John Menzies of Comrie.

No. 9 Company.

Captain Dougal Campbell of Craignish. Retired in 1745.
Lieutenant John Mackneil.
Ensign Gordon Graham of Draines.[3]

No. 10 Company.

Captain John Monro of Newmore. Promoted to be Lt. Col. 1743; retired 1749.
Lieutenant Francis Grant, son of the Laird of Grant.[4] Died Lieut.-General 1782.
Ensign Edward Carrick.
Surgeon George Monro.
Quarter Master John Forbes.
Chaplain Hon. Gideon Murray.
Adjutant John Lindsay.[5]

---

1. Stewart of Garth calls him Dougal Campbell, but he appears as James in his commission.
2. It is not stated to which companies Lieutenant Malcolm Fraser and Francis Grant belonged. No other lieutenants are mentioned for Balliemore and Newmore; they have therefore been assigned respectively to them.
3. i. e. Drynie. A younger son of the Laird.
4. See note to Lieutenant Malcolm Fraser.
5. Garth gives the adjutant as being Gilbert Stewart (presumably the ensign to the Colonel's Company.) He probably acted in this capacity until John Lindsay was gazetted to the regiment.

L

OFFICERS OF THE 42ND ROYAL HIGHLAND REGIMENT AS COPIED FROM THE BRITISH ARMY LIST, PUBLISHED 20TH JUNE, 1759.

Col. Lord Jno. Murray, Lt. Gen.

Lt. Col. Francis Grant.
Major Gordon Graham.
Capt. John Reid.
Capt. John McNeil.
Capt. Allan Campbell.
Capt. Thomas Graeme.
Capt. James Abercrombie.
Capt. John Campbell.
Capt. James Stewart.
Capt. James Murray.
Capt. Thomas Stirling.
Capt. Francis McLean.
Capt. Archibald Campbell.
Capt. Alexander St. Clair.
Capt. William Murray.
Capt. John Stuart.
Capt. Alexander Reid.
Capt. William Grant.
Capt. David Haldane.
Capt. Lieut. Robert Gray.
Lieut. John Campbell.
Lieut. Kenneth Tolme.
Lieut. James Grant.
Lieut. John Graham.
Lieut. Alex. Turnbull.
Lieut. Alex. Campbell.
Lieut. Alex. McIntosh.
Lieut. James Gray.
Lieut. John Small.
Lieut. Arch. Campbell, Sen.
Lieut. James Campbell.
Lieut. Archibald Lamont.

Lieut. Gordon Clunes.
Lieut. James Fraser.
Lieut. John Robertson.
Lieut. John Grant.
Lieut. George Leslie.
Lieut. Duncan Campbell.
Lieut. Adam Stuart.
Lieut. Donald Campbell.
Lieut. George Grant.
Lieut. James McIntosh.
Lieut. Robert Robertson.
Lieut. John Smith.
Lieut. Peter Grant.
Lieut. Alex. Farquharson.
Lieut. John Campbell, Jr.
Lieut. George Sinclair.
Ensign Elbert Herring.
Ensign William Brown.
Ensign Thomas Fletcher.
Ensign Alex. Donaldson.
Ensign William McIntosh.
Ensign Patrick Sinclair.
Ensign Archibald Campbell, Jun
Ensign John Gregor.
Ensign Lewis Grant.
Ensign Archibald Campbell, Sen
Ensign John Graham.
Ensign Allen Grant.
Ensign John Leith.
Ensign Charles Menzies.
Ensign Archibald McNab.
Ensign John Chas. St. Clair.

Lieut. David Mills.　　　　Ensign John Gordon.
Lieut. Simon Blair.　　　　Ensign Neil McLean.
Lieut. David Barclay.　　　Ensign Thomas Cunison.
Lieut. Archibald Campbell, Jr. Sergt. Phineas McPherson.
Lieut. Alex Mackay.　　　　Chaplain James Stewart.
Lieut. Robert Menzies.　　Adj. James Grant.
Lieut. Patrick Balneavis.　Aldj. Alex McLean.
Lieut. John Campbell, Sen.　Quarter Master John Graham.
Lieut. Alex. McLean.　　　Quarter Master Adam Stewart.
Lieut. George Sinclair.　　Surgeon David Hepburn.
Lieut. John Murray.　　　Surgeon Robt. Drummond.

Agt., Mr. Drummond, Spring Garden.

The following corrections were interlined in ink in the above Army List of 1759, which was found in the British Museum:

Capt. John Reid was made Major. Aug. 5, 1759.
Capt. John Campbell, removed to the 17th.
Capt. David Haldane, removed to a Regiment at Jamaica.
Lieut. Alexander McLean, made captain of corps of Highlanders.
Lieut. George Sinclair, dead.
Lieut. George Sinclair, removed to Crawford's Regiment.
Ensign Thomas Fletcher, made lieutenant June 1, 1759.
Ensign William McIntosh, removed to Keith's Corps.
Sergt. Phineas McPherson, made ensign June 1, 1759.
Lauchlan Johnson, made chaplain 20th August, 1759, in place of James Stewart.
Alexander Donaldson, made adjutant 20th March, 1759, in place of Alexander McLean.

M

REFERENCES TO THE BLACK WATCH IN THE 1759 CAMPAIGN TAKEN FROM "COMMISSARY WILSON'S ORDERLY BOOK."

Albany, 22 May, 1759. Two companies of the Royal Highland Regiment are also to receive batteaux and load them with provision and baggage. A sergeant and 12 men of the Rhode Island Regiment are to relieve a party of the Royal Highland Regiment at the Half-Way House on the way to Schenectady; they are to march tomorrow morning and carry six days' provision with them.

Albany, 23d May, 1759. Three captains of the Royal Highlanders summoned among others to a general Court Martial, of which Col. Francis Grant was President, to set tomorrow at the Town House in Albany at 3 o'clock to try all prisoners that may be brought before them.

Albany, 26th May, 1759. An officer and 25 men of the Royal Highland Regiment with a week's provision to be sent this afternoon to Widow McGinnes House to protect settlement; one Company of the Royal Highland Regiment to march tomorrow morning at 5 o'clock; they will take their tents and camp equipage with them, for which a wagon will be allowed on sending to Col. Bradstreet for it; the officer commanding that company to call upon the General this night. The General Court Martial of which Col. Grant is President to meet again tomorrow at 8 o'clock.

Albany, 31st May, 1759. The Royal Highland Regiment to march tomorrow morning at 5 o'clock to Halfmoon, where they will take the artillery under their charge and escort the same to Fort Edward.

Fort Edward, 6th June, 1759. Lieut. Col. Robinson will mark out the Camp tomorrow morning at 5 o'clock that the Regiments may take up their ground as they arrive; the Regiments to encamp * * * Royal Highlanders on the right. A Serj. and 16 men of ye Royal Highlanders to take the General's Guard.

Fort Edward, 7th June, 1759. The Regiments are not to change their encampment until the ground be quite dry.

Fort Edward, 8th June, 1759. The Regiments to change their encampment this day at 12 o'clock.

Fort Edward, 9th June, 1759. Field Officer for the Picquit tomorrow, Major Graham. The Light infantry of the Highland Regiment is to practice firing ball tomorrow morning at 6 o'clock, near the Royal Block House on the other side of the river.

The Royal Highland Regiment to furnish 2 captains, 6 subs., and 200 men * * * ; this detachment to take batteaux tomorrow morning at day break. The Royal Highland Regiment to take 20 batteaux, and 60 of the 200 men with arms to serve as a covering party. The whole to take provisions for tomorrow with them; they are to proceed to Col. Haviland's Camp, opposite to Fort Miller, where the commanding officer will apply to Col. Haviland who will order the batteaux to be immediately loaded, that the whole party may return to Fort Edward without loss of time.

Fort Edward, 10th June, 1759. Field Officer for the Picquit this night Major (Gordon) Graham, for tomorrow Major (Allen) Campbell, Colonel of the day, Col. (Francis) Grant. Two captains of the Royal Highlanders to sit with others in General Court Martial tomorrow morning at 8 o'clock, to try such prisoners as are on the Provost Guard. The Royal Highlanders and Montgomery's Regiments to send as many men this afternoon at 4 o'clock as are necessary to clean the ground where the Light Infantry is to encamp. They will receive axes on applying to the store-keeper in the Fort,. which they will return when they have finished that work.

Fort Edward, 11th June, 1759. Colo. of the day, Col. Grant, Field Officer of the Picquits, Major Campbell.

Fort Edward, 12th June, 1759. Block Houses to be relieved tomorrow by the Line * * * the one joining the east side of the Bridge by 1 Sub., 2 Serjts., 2 corpls. and 24 men of the Royal Highlanders; the one in the front of the Right of the Royal, one Serjt., one Corpl. and 10 men of the Royal Highlanders.

Fort Edward, 13th June, 1759. The Royal Highland Regiment to strick their tents tomorrow at Revallie Beating. The Royal Highlanders posted in their Block Houses as per ordered of yesterday, to be relieved immediately.

Fort Edward, 17th June. The First Battalion Massachusetts to strike their tents at Revallie Beating and march half an hour after to the Halfway Brook where the commanding officer will put himself under the command of Col. Grant.

Fort Edward, 19th June, 1759. The Royal Highlanders will furnish one Sub. and 30 men towards the working party required tomorrow to repair the roads.

Fort Edward, 20th June. Capt. Campbell of the Royal Highland Grenediers is appointed Major to the Battalion of Grenediers for the Campaign.

Lake George, 22d June, 1759. The Royal Highlanders to receive one day's fresh beef tomorrow.

Lake George 24th June. Field Officer for tomorrow, Major Graham.

Lake George, 26th June, 1759. The Royal Highlanders to receive 7 days' provisions tomorrow.

Lake George, 27th June. Generals Guard tomorrow, Royal Highlanders. 2 Companies of Grenediers with 2 Companies of Light Infantry ordered this morning with as many Rangers and Indians as Maj. Rogers can furnish, the whole commanded by Maj. Campbell, to march tomorrow two hours before daybreak by the same route Col. Haviland took; which post Capt. Johnson will show, and to remain there whilst the boats are fishing. They are to take one day's provisions and to go as light as possible as they are not only a covering party to the boats, but to attack any body of the enemy they may find.

Lake George, 5th July, 1759. A General Court Martial to set tomorrow morning at the President's Tent at 8 o'clock for the trial of a man suspected of robbery * * * Major Graham and two captains of the Royal Highlanders to attend.

Lake George 8th July, 1759. The Royal Highlanders will take the Gen's Guard tomorrow half an hour after 4.

Lake George, 11th July, 1759. Capt. John Campbell of the Royal Highlanders is appointed Major in the late Forbes, and is to be obeyed as such. Royal Highlanders to receive 35 batteaux. Oars and whatever else belongs to the batteaux will be delivered at the same time. Each batteaux will carry 12 barrels of flour or 9 of pork when ordered to load, and it is supposed will have about 20 men or a few more in each battoe.

Lake George, 12th July. A General Court Martial of the Regulars to be held tomorrow morning at 6 o'clock. Col. Grant President, Major John Campbell to attend.

Lake George, 13th July. Colonel of the Day tomorrow, Col. Grant. Field Officer tomorrow night, Major Graham. Generals Guard tomorrow, Royal Highlanders. The General Court Martial of which Col. Grant was President, is dissolved. Royal Highland-

ers to receive a proportion of flour for five days wihch they are
to get baked tomorrow and keep.

Lake George, 19th July, 1759. The Royal Highlanders one of
the Regiments appointed to sit in general Court Martial tomorrow
at 6 o'clock. The Regiments to load their batteaux tomorrow
morning beginning at 5 o'clock in the following manner, Montgomery's Pork, Royal Highlanders, Flour, * * * two regiments to load
at a time, one flour and one pork, and to be allowed an hour for
loading, and when loaded to return to their stations.

Lake George, 20th July, 1759. For the day this day, Regulars,
Col. Grant. On landing the Col. Grant to take the command of
the late Forbes' Brigade.

Camp near Ticonderoga, 22d July. For the Picquit tomorrow
night, Major Graham.

Camp before Ticonderoga, 23d July, 1759. Collo. of the day
tomorrow, Collo. Grant. Field Officer of the Picquits this night,
Major Graham.

Camp at Ticonderoga, 24th July, 1759. Serjt. Murray of the
Royal Highland Regiment is appointed to oversee people making
Fasciens, and to keep an account of the number made.

Camp at Ticonderoga, 25th July, 1759. The following car-
penters * * * James Frazer, George McDougall, James Frazer, John
McColme, John Robinson, James Cumming, and James McDonald
of the Royal Highlanders to be at the sawmills tomorrow at 5
o'clock and if Capt. Loreing should not be there they will receive
their directions from Brigadier Ruggles.

The Royal Highland Regiment to draw tomorrow early two
days bisquit and two days pork, bisquit in lieu of flour, which
completes them to the 28th inclusive.

Ticonderoga, 26th July, 1759. Adjutant for the day tomorrow
Royal Highlands.

Ticonderoga, 28th July, 1759. A General Court Martial of the
line to be held at the President's tent at 8 o'clock tomorrow morn-

ing. Col. Grant, President, two Majors and ten Captains, two of whom were from the Royal Highlanders.

Ticonderoga, 29th July, 1759. The ovens to be given for the use of troops in the following manner:— * * * No. 2 to the Inniskilling and Royal Highlanders. No bakers but such as those Corps imploy to make in any of those ovens. The Royal Highland Regiments to strick their tents and march immediately to the Landing Place, and they will send their tents and baggage in batteaux.

Ticonderoga, 1st August, 1759. As a number of shoes are come up, intended for the use of the Army, and will be delivered to them at the prime cost in England, which three shillings and six pence per pair. The Regiments may receive in the following manner and proportion, or as many of that proportion as they like to take by applying to Mr. Tucker, agent to Mr. Kilby at the Landing Place. Royal Highlanders 366.

Capt. Reid is appointed Major to the Royal Highland Regiment.

Crown Point, 5th August, 1759. Collo. of the day tomorrow Regulars Collo. Grant; Field officer for the Picquits tomorrow night Maj. Reid.

Crown Point, 6th August, 1759. Adjutant of the day tomorrow Royal Highlanders. As twenty-four barrels of Spruce beer is come to the fort the corps may send for it immediately in the following proportions * * * Royal Highlanders, three barrels.

Crown Point, 7th August, 1759. Corporal Sinclair of the Highlanders and Parceloo of the Inniskilling Regiment with 16 leabours used to digging to attend Lieut. Gray Tomorrow at 5 o'clock; the evening gun is the signal for the working party to leave of work.

Crown Point, 8th August, 1759. The Regulars to receive 4 days provisions tomorrow of pork, beginning at Revallie Beating by Forbes followed by Royal Highlanders, etc. It is concluded that they have their bread from Ticonderoga as was ordered.

Crown Point, 10th August, 1759. Ens. Gregor of the Royal Highlanders * * * are appointed overseers of the works that are carrying on at the fort. They will attend Lieut. Col. Eyre tomorrow morning at 5 o'clock and follow such directions as they shall receive from him.

Crown Point, 11th August, 1759. Collo. of the day tomorrow, Collo. Grant. For the building of the fort the following quarriers * * * five of the Royal Highlanders * * * to attend Lieut. Col. Eyre tomorrow morning at the hour of work, and are to continue daily to work as quarriers.

Crown Point, 12th August, 1759. Adjutant of the Day tomorrow, Royal Highlanders.

Crown Point, 14th August, 1759. Field officer for the work tomorrow, Major Reid.

Crown Point, 15th August. 1759. The following Surgeons Mates are to join the Regiments and serve as Mates in room of Officers serving as such; Mr. Goldthwat an additional Mate in the Royal Highlanders to be put on the establishment of Forbe's, Mr. Carter to the Royal Highlanders.

Crown Point, 16th August, 1759. The following sawiers are to attend Lieut. Col. Eyre tomorrow at 5 o'clock: * * * Royal Highlanders, Robert Kennedy, John McFarling and Robert Bain. The following masons are likewise to attend Lieut. Col. Eyre tomorrow morning at 5 o'clock: * * * Royal Highlanders, Dougal McKeafter and John Stewart. The above artificers are to work daily and to follow such directions as they shall receive from Lieut. Col. Eyre.

Crown Point, 17th August, 1759. Collo. of the day tomorrow, Collo. Grant. The following masons to attend Lieut. Col. Eyre tomorrow morning at five o'clock; * * * Royal Highlanders Angus McDonald and William Milligan.

Crown Point, 18th August, 1759. Adjutant of the day tomorrow, Royal Highlanders.

Crown Point, 24th Aug., 1759. Adjutant of the day, tomorrow, Royal Highlanders.

Crown Point, 27th August, 1759. The following soldiers to attend Lieut. Eyre tomorrow morning at 5 o'clock and to take their directions from him; Royal Highlanders, John Fraser, John Mc-Elvore, James Bruce, Allex'r Sutherland.

Crown Point, 28th Aug. Field Officer of the work tomorrow-Major Reid.

Crown Point, 30 August, 1759. Adjutant of the day, Royal Highlanders.

Crown Point, 1st Sept. Collo. of the day, tomorrow, Collo. Grant.

Crown Point, 3d September, 1759. John McNeal, Grenadier in Royal Highland Regiment, * * * to attend Lieut. Col. Eyre this day at 12 o'clock and to follow such directions as he shall give.

Crown Point, 4th Sept., 1759. Collo. of the day, tomorrow, Collo. Grant. Field Officer for the work, Major Reid. The men of the Royal Highland Regiment who have been employed in making baskets will be paid for the same by the Quartermaster's applying to Mr. Gray this afternoon after the work is over. The Regiments to receive tomorrow morning two pounds of fresh meat and one pound of rice for the number of men set opposite the names of each corps, and the Regiments are to apply said fresh beef and rice entirely for the use of the sick. Royal Highlanders 22.

Crown Point, 5th Sept., 1759. Field Officer for the works tomorrow, Major Reid. Adjutant of the day, tomorrow, Royal Highlanders. Allex'r Forbes of the Royal Highlanders, mason, to accompany Lieut. Col. Eyre tomorrow and follow such directions as he shall give.

Crown Point, 6th Sept. Serjt. Clark of the Royal Highlanders to be one of the four sergeants to attend the works daily and to receive directions from Lieut. Col. Eyre.

Crown Point, 7th Sept. For the day, tomorrow, Collo. Grant.

Crown Point, 11th Sept. Adjutant of the day tomorrow, Royal Highlanders. A general court martial of the Regulars to sit tomorrow at the President's Tent at 8 o'clock; Collo. Foster, President, Major John Campbell, Major Reid, * * one captain of the Royal Highlanders.

Crown Point, 12th Sept. A detachment of 100 Grenadiers, 30 of the Light Infantry of Regiments, non-commissioned officers in proportion to be commanded by a captain of the Grenadiers and 2 Subalterns of each Corps to parade tomorrow at Revallie beating on the left of the front of the light infantry and to take 30 batteaux to Ticonderoga where he is to apply to the Commissary and load 15 with 30 barrels of flour in each batteaux, the other 15 with 16 barrels of pork each. The Royal Highland Regiment to furnish the batteaux and the captain commanding the party will see them this night that they may be ready to set off at Revallie beating and to return as soon as they are loaded.

Crown Point, 15th Sept., 1759. For the day tomorrow, Collo. Grant. Field Officer for the Picquits this night, Regulars Major Reid. Field Officer for the works tomorrow, Major John Campbell.

Crown Point, 16th Sept., 1759. Field Officer for the works tomorrow, Major Reid.

Crown Point, 17th Sept. Adjutant of the day tomorrow, Royal Highlanders.

Crown Point, 18th Sept., 1759. For the day tomorrow, Collo. Grant.

Crown Point, 21st Sept., 1759. For the day tomorrow, Collo. Grant. For the Picquits this night, Major Reid. Field Officer for the works tomorrow, Major John Campbell.

Crown Point, 23d Sept., 1759. Adjutant of the day tomorrow, Royal Highlanders.

Crown Point, 25th Sept. Lieut. Tolmey of the Royal Highlanders is appointed Overseer for the work on the fort and to receive his directions from Leiut. Col. Eyre.

Crown Point, 26th Sept., 1759. Field officer for the Picquits this night, Major John Campbell; tomorrow night, Major Reid.

LORD HOWE MONUMENT. (TROUT BROOK) TICONDEROGA. N. Y.

AT TICONDEROGA

Boulder in Academy Park to the Heroes of the Four Nations—Indian, French, British and American who fought at Ticonderoga.

Monument marking the spot at the mouth of Trout Brook, where Lord Howe was supposed to have fallen.

(Both Boulder and Monument were erected by the late Rev. Joseph Cook)

Crown Point, 27th Sept., 1759. For the day tomorrow, Collo. Grant. Field Officer for the Picquits this night, Major Reid.

Crown Point, 29th Sept. Adjutant for the day tomorrow, Royal Highlanders.

Crown Point, 30th Sept., 1759. Collo. for the day tomorrow, Collo. Grant.

Crown Point, 2d Oct., 1759. Field Officer for the Picquits this night, Major John Campbell; tomorrow night, Major Reid.

Crown Point, 3d October. For the day tomorrow, Collo. Grant. Field Officer for the Picquits this night, Major Reid. Field Officer for the works tomorrow, John Campbell. A General Court martial of the Regulars to sit at the President's tent tomorrow at 9 o'clock * * * two captains of the Royal Highlanders.

Crown Point, 5th Oct., 1759. Adjutant of the day tomorrow, Royal Highlanders.

Crown Point, 6th Oct., 1759. For the day tomorrow, Collo. Grant. The regular regiments to give in their cartridges that are damaged this day to the artillery and to receive as much powder, paper, ball and twine as will compleat their ammunition. The Royal Highlanders 475.

Crown Point, 7th October. The Regiments to prepare their batteaux to the following numbers and to have their sails fixed according to patern Col. Haviland approved of; * * * Royal Highlanders 24, * * *

Crown Point, 8th October. Royal Highlanders are to take two batteaux more than what were ordered yesterday.

Crown Point, 9th October. For the day tomorrow, Collo. Grant. Field Officer for Picquits this night, Major Reid. The undermentioned Corps are to send a batteaux each at Retreat beating to Ticonderoga to receive tomorrow morning the following number of loaves weighing six pounds and a half each; they are to pay to the person Gen. Lyman appoints to receive the money the following sums being one penny sterling for baking seven pounds of flour: Royal Highlanders 460 loaves, 1; 7; 8 Sterling. * * *

The Royal Highlanders are to leave Subaltern Officer each, exclusive of officers employed as overseers at the King's Works, with three Sergeants, three Corp'ls each with the men that are left behind; when the Regiments march, the officers and men of each corps will encamp on the Center of the encampment of the Corps * * * and a sentry to be kept in the encampment that nothing may be spoiled or taken away during the absence of the Regiment. The Regiments are to give the following numbers for the Brig and Sloop and will send seamen if they have them: For the Brig, * * Royal Highlanders 14 men.

Crown Point, 11th Oct., 1759. Adjutant of the day tomorrow, Royal Highlanders.

Lake Shamplaine, 15th Oct., 1759. For the day tomorrow, Collo. Grant.

Ligonier Bay, 14th Oct., 1759. Field Officer for the Picquit this night, Major John Campbell; tomorrow night, Major Reid.

Lake Shamplaine, 15th Oct., 1759. For the day tomorrow, Collo. Grant. Field Officer for the Picquits this night, Major Reid.

Camp at Schuylers Island, 18th Oct., 1759. For the day tomorrow, Collo. Grant.

Crown Point, 22nd Oct., 1759. Adjutant of the day tomorrow, Royal Highlanders.

Crown Point, 25th October. 22 men of the Royal Highlanders are to be sent to the Hospital at Fort Edward. * * The surgeon cf the Royal Highlanders is to attend them to Fort Edward, a Corporal and 6 men of the Royal Highlanders with one batteaux * * * are to convey the sick to the Sawmills, where the officer will leave the batteau with Lieut. Col. Miller and march the sick to the Landing Place.

Crown Point, 27th Oct., 1759. For the day tomorrow, Collo. Grant. Field Officer for the Picquits this night, Major Reid.

Crown Point, 28th Oct., 1759. Adjutant for the day tomorrow, Royal Highlanders.

Crown Point, 30th October. Officer for the day, tomorrow, Collo. Grant. A General Court martial to be held at the President's Tent tomorrow at 9 o'clock to try all such prisoners as shall be brought before them; Col. Grant, President, * * * One Captain of the Royal Highlanders.

Crown Point, 31st Oct., 1759. Field Officer for the Picquits this night, Major Reid. The General Court martial of which Collo. Grant was President is dissolved; the Prisoners of the Royal Highland Regiment is acquitted.

Crown Point, 1st Nov., 1759. For the day tomorrow, Collo. Grant.

Crown Point, 3d Nov., 1759. For the Picquits tomorrow night, Major John Campbell; for the works tomorrow, Major John Campbell; Adjutant of the day tomorrow, Royal Highlanders.

N

COLONEL ROGER TOWNSHEND.

Roger Townshend, fifth son of Charles Viscount Townshend, and younger brother of Gen'l George Townshend (afterwards 4th Viscount and 1st Marquis) to whom Quebec surrendered when Wolfe was killed, was commissioned Lieutenant-Colonel 1st Feb., 1758, and served as Adjutant-General in the Expedition against Louisbourg, and Deputy Adjutant-General in this Campaign with Rank of Colonel. He was killed in the Trenches before Ticonderoga by a cannon ball on the 25th July, 1759. and his remains were transmitted to Albany for interment. His spirit and military knowledge justly entitled him to the esteem of every soldier; and accordingly the loss of him was universally lamented.

Knox I, 360, 289, 401, 403.
Wilson's Orderly Book, page 77.

Supplement to the New York Mercury, Tuesday, July 31, 1759.

Extract from a letter dated Albany, July 29, 1759.

"The same evening (July 27), an Express arrived from Ticonderoga, with an account of Colonel Townshend being killed, in reconnoitering the Fort, by a cannon ball.

* * * * * *

Yesterday about 12 o'clock, Colonel Townshend's corpse arrived here, and was decently interred."

In the "Church Book" St. Peter's, Albany, appears the following entry:

1759 July 30   To cash received for braking ground in the
                 church to lay the body of Coll. Townson........ £5/0/0
                 To cash ret for Paull... 9

The following is a copy of the inscription on the monument to Col. Townshend in Westminster Abbey

"This Monument was erected
By a disconsolate Parent
The Lady Viscountess Townshend
To the Memory of her Fifth Son
The Hon'ble Lieut. Colonel Roger Townshend
who was killed by a Cannon Ball
on the 25th of July, 1759, in the 28th year of his age
as he was reconnoitering ye French lines at Ticonderoga
In North America
From the Parent the Brother and the Friend
His sociable and amiable manners
His enterprizing Bravery
And the Integrity of His Heart
May claim the tribute of affliction
Yet Stranger weep not
For tho' premature His Death
His life was glorious
Enrolling Him with the names
of those Immortal Statesmen and Commanders
Whose wisdom and Intrepidity
In the course of this Comprehensive and Successful War
Have Extended the Commerce
And upheld the Majesty of these Kingdoms
Beyond the idea of any former age."

Monument to Lieut. Colonel Roger Townshend in Westminster Abbey
(The Bayonet on Monument found on battlefield of Ticonderoga and
placed on memorial by Dean Stanley)

The following is an extract from a letter from the head verger of Westminster Abbey

"I should like to draw your attention to the broken bayonet in the upper part of the Townshend monument. It is a relic of the struggle between the French and English in North America and it comes from Ticonderoga and may have been used in that particular 'march to Ticonderoga, where Col. Townshend was killed.' It was given to Dean Stanley when in America and he fixed it on the monument as he did the wreath of leaves on the monument of Major Andre.

Lord Eversley, who when H. M. first Commissioner of Works was the Rt. Hon. J. G. Shaw Lefevre—is much struck by the Townshend inscription, especially the latter part, which, he has told me, is worthy of Edmund Burke and which I know he would like to attribute to that great orator and statesman."

O

BIBLIOGRAPHY.

A Military History of Perthshire, 1660-1902. Edited by the Marchioness of Tullibardine. Perth R. A. & J. Hay, 1908.

Chronicles of the Atholl and Tullibardine Families. Collected and arranged by John, Seventh Duke of Atholl, K. T., in Five Volumes. Ballantyle Press, 1908.

Sketches of the Character, Manners and Present State of the Highlanders of Scotland, with details of the Military Service of the Highland Regiments, by Colonel David Stewart (of Garth), Edinburgh. Archibald, Constable & Co., 1822.

The Scottish Highlands, Highland Clans and Regiments, by John S. Keltie, F. S. A. S. Edinburgh, A. Fullerton & Co.

The Regimental Records of the British Army, by John S. Farmer, London, Grant Richards, 1901.

An Historical Account of the Settlements of Scotch Highlanders in America, etc., by J. P. MacLean, Ph. D. Cleveland, The Helmar-Taylor Co., Glasgow, John MacKay, 1900.

Historical Record of the 42nd or Royal Highland Regiment of Foot, 1729-1844. Illustrated. London, Parker, 1845.

Historical Record of the 73rd Regiment, 1780-1851. Illustrated. London. Parker, 1851.

Chronology and Book of Days of the 42nd Royal Highlanders, The Black Watch, 1729-1905. Berwick-on-Tweed, Martin's Printing Works, 1906.

History of Black Watch. Johnston, 1893.

The Black Watch. The Record of an Historic Regiment, by Archibald Forbes, LL. D. Cassell & Co., 1910.

Black Watch Episode of the Year 1731, by H. D. MacWilliam. Johnston, 1908.

Short History of the Black Watch, 1725-1907. Blackwood, 1908.

The Official Records of the Mutiny in the Highland Regiment (The Black Watch), A London Incident of the Year 1743, by H. D. MacWilliam. Johnston, 1910.

Legends of the Black Watch, by James Grant, Routledge, 1904.

Knox's Journal.

Brown's Highland Clans.

Beaston's Naval and Military Memoirs.

A Biographical Dictionary of Eminent Scotsmen. Chambers. Glasgow, 1832-35.

Pennsylvania Colonial Records.

Correspondence of William Pitt when Secretary of State, with Colonial Governors, etc., by Gertrude Selwyn Kimball. MacMillian, 1906.

Commissary Wilson's Orderly Book. Expedition of the British and Provincial Army under Maj. Gen. Jeffrey Amherst, against Ticonderoga and Crown Point, 1759. Albany, J. Munsell. London, Trubner Co., 1857.

New York Colonial Manuscript, by Broadhead, Weed, Parsons & Co., Albany, 1856.

History of Canada.   Translated from L'Histoire du Canada by F. X. Garneau, by Andrew Bell.   Richard Worthington & Son, Montreal, 1866.

Illustrated Histories of the Scottish Regiments by Lieut. Colonel Percy Groves.   Illustrated by Harry Payne.   Edinburgh, 1893.

The Regimental Records of the 1st and 2nd Battalions The Black Watch.

The Regimental Records of the Perthshire Militia, now the 3rd Battalion, The Black Watch.

Cannon's Official History of the 42nd, 1729-1844.

Cannon's Official History of the 73rd, 1779-1850.

The Annual Register.

Records and Badges of the British Army.   Chichester.

Standards and Colors of the Army.   Milne.

War Medals of the British Army.   Carter and Long.

The Black Watch.   Andrew Picken.

Reminiscences of a Campaign.   John Malcolm, 42nd.

Retrospect of a Military Life.   Q. M. S. Anton, 42nd.

Fontenoy, The Campaign of.   Skrine.

Mangalore, The Siege of.   By an Officer Present.

Recollections of a Military Life.   Sergeant Morris, 73rd.

Military Reminiscences (Polygar Campaigns).   Colonel Welsh.

Five Years in Kaffirland (Second War).   Mrs. Ward.

Campaigning in Kaffirland.

The 5th Regiment Royal Scots of Canada.   Captain Chambers.

History of the British Army.   J. W. Fortescue.

Memoirs of Sergeant Donald Macleod. Late 42nd.

Reminiscences of a Veteran. Alexander Robb, Late 42nd.

P

The British Army.

Milne in "Standards and Colors of the Army," says that the British Army as a permanent force dates from 26 January 1660-61. Charles II established three troops of Life Guards—one of Horse (subsequently Royal Horse Guards Blue), the King's Royal Regiment of Guards (now Grenadier Guards), and the Duke of Albemarle's Regiment of Foot (now Coldstream Guards.)

The Present Establishment:

1. The Cavalry.

The First Life Guards, The Second Life Guards, The Royal Horse Guards (The Blues), The First (The King's) Dragoon Guards, The Second Dragoon Guards (Queen's Bays), The Third (The Prince of Wales's) Dragoon Guards. The Fourth (Royal Irish Dragoon Guards, The Fifth (Princess Charlotte of Wales's) Dragoon Guards, The Sixth Dragoon Guards (Carabiniers), The Seventh (The Princess Royal's) Dragoon Guards, The First (Royal) Dragoons, The Second Dragoons (Royal Scots Greys), The Third (The King's Own) Hussars, The Fourth (The Queen's Own) Hussars, The Fifth (Royal Irish) Lancers, The Sixth (Inniskilling) Dragoons, The Seventh (The Queen's Own)) Hussars, The Eighth (The King's Royal Irish) Hussars, The Ninth (The Queen's Royal) Lancers, The Tenth (The Prince of Wales' Own Royal) Hussars, The Eleventh (Prince Albert's Own) Hussars, The Twelfth (The Prince of Wales's Royal) Lancers, The Thirteenth Hussars, The Fourteenth (The King's) Hussars, The Fifteenth (The King's) Hussars, The Sixteenth (The Queen's) Lancers, The Seventeenth (The Duke of Cambridge's Own) Lancers, The Eighteenth Hussars, The Nineteenth (Princess of Wales's Own) Hussars, The Twentieth Hussars, The Twenty-first (Empress of India's) Lancers.

11. The Royal Artillery.

The Royal Regiment of Artillery.

The Memorial Tablet to the Black Watch of 1758 and its Major, Duncan Campbell of Inverawe, erected on the Battle Ground of July 8, 1758

(Frederick B. Richards at side of Monument reading inscription on the QUAICH presented to him by the Campbells of Inverawe).

III.   The Royal Engineers.
      The Corps of Royal Engineers.

IV.   The Foot Guards.

      The Grenadier Guards, The Coldstream Guards, The Scots Guards, The Irish Guards.

V.   Territorial Regiments (Regiments of Foot).

The Royal Scots (Lothian Regiment), formerly The 1st.

The Queen's (Royal West Surrey Regiment), formerly The 2nd.

The Buffs (East Kent Regiment), formerly The 3rd.

The King's Own (Royal Lancaster Regiment), formerly The 4th.

The Northumberland Fusiliers, formerly The 5th.

The Royal Warwickshire Regiment, formerly The 6th.

The Royal Fusiliers (City of London Regiment), formerly The 7th.

The King's (Liverpool Regiment), formerly The 8th.

The Norfolk Regiment, formerly The 9th.

The Lincolnshire Regiment, formerly The 10th.

The Devonshire Regiment, formerly The 11th.

The Suffolk Regiment, formerly The 12th.

The Prince Albert's (Somersetshire Light Infantry), formerly The 13th.

The Prince of Wales's Own (West Yorkshire Regiment), formerly The 14th.

The East Yorkshire Regiment, formerly The 15th.

The Bedfordshire Regiment, formerly The 16th.

The Leicestershire Regiment, formerly The 17th.

The Royal Irish Regiment, formerly The 18th.

The Princess of Wales's Own (Yorkshire Regiment), formerly The 19th.

The Lancashire Fusiliers, formerly The 20th (East Devonshire).

The Royal Scots Fusiliers, formerly The 21st.

The Cheshire Regiment, formerly The 22nd.

The Royal Welsh Fusiliers, formerly The 23rd.

The South Wales Borderers, formerly The 24th. (2nd Warwickshire).

The King's Own Scottish Borderers, formerly The 25th.

The Cameronians (Scottish Rifles)

    1st Batt., formerly The 26th.

    2nd Batt., formerly The 90th. (Perthshire Volunteers—Light Infantry).

The Royal Inniskilling Fusiliers, 1st Batt., formerly The 27th.

    2nd Batt., formerly The 108th (Madras Infantry).

The Gloucestershire Regiment, 1st. Batt., formerly The 28th (North Gloucestershire).

    2nd Batt., formerly The 61st (South Gloucestershire).

The Worcestershire Regiment, 1st Batt., formerly The 29th.

    2nd Batt., Formerly The 36th (Herefordshire).

The East Lancashire Regiment, 1st Batt., formerly The 30th (Cambridgeshire).

    2nd Batt., formerly The 59th (2nd Nottinghamshire).

The East Surrey Regiment, 1st Batt., formerly The 31st (Huntingdonshire).

    2nd Batt., formerly The 70th (Surrey).

Duke of Cornwall's Light Infantry, 1st Batt., formerly The 32nd.

    2nd Batt., formerly The 46th (South Devonshire).

The Duke of Wellington's (West Riding Regiment) 1st Batt., formerly The 33rd.

2nd Batt., formerly The 76th.

The Border Regiment, 1st Batt. formerly The 34th (Cumberland). 2nd Batt., formerly The 55th (Westmoreland).

The Royal Sussex Regiment, 1st Batt., formerly The 35th. 2nd Batt., formerly The 10th (Bengal Infantry).

The Hampshire Regiment, 1st Batt., formerly The 37th. 2nd Batt., formerly The 67th (South Hampshire).

The South Staffordshire Regiment, 1st Batt., formerly The 38th (1st Staffordshire). 2nd Batt., formerly The 80th (Staffordshire Volunteers).

The Dorsetshire Regiment, 1st Batt., formerly The 39th. 2nd Batt., formerly The 54th (West Norfolk).

The Prince of Wales's Volunteers (South Lancashire Regiment, 1st Batt., formerly The 40th (2nd Somersetshire); 2nd Batt., formerly The 82nd.

The Welsh Regiment, 1st Batt., formerly The 41st; 2nd Batt., formerly The 69th (South Lincolnshire).

The Black Watch (Royal Highlanders) 1st Batt., formerly The 42nd; 2nd Batt., formerly The 73rd (Perthshire).

The Oxfordshire Light Infantry, 1st Batt., formerly The 43rd (Monmouthshire Light Infantry), 2nd Batt., formerly The 52nd.

The Essex Regiment, 1st Batt., formerly The 44th; 2nd Batt., The 56th (West Essex).

The Sherwood Foresters (Derbyshire Regiment), 1st Batt., formerly the 45th (Nottinghamshire); 2nd Batt., The 95th (Derbyshire).

The Royal North Lancashire Regiment, 1st Batt., formerly The 47th (Lancashire); 2nd Batt., formerly The 81st (Loyal Lincoln Volunteers).

The Northamptonshire Regiment, 1st Batt., formerly The 48th; 2nd Batt., formerly The 58th (Rutlandshire).

Princess Charlotte of Wales's (Royal Berkshire Regiment), 1st

Batt., formerly The 49th (Hertfordshire); 2 Batt., formerly
The 66th (Berkshire).

The Queen's Own (Royal West Kent) Regiment, 1st Batt., formerly

The 50th 2nd Batt., formerly The 97th (The Earl of Ulster's).

The King's Own Yorkshire Light Infantry, 1st Batt., formerly The
51st (2nd Yorkshire West Riding); 2nd Batt., The 105th
(Madras Light Infantry).

The King's (Shropshire Light Infantry) 1st Batt., formerly The
53rd; 2nd Batt., formerly The 85th (Bucks Volunteers).

The Duke of Cambridge's Own (Middlesex Regiment), 1st Batt.,
formerly The 57th (West Middlesex); 2nd Batt., formerly
The 77th (East Middlesex).

The King's Royal Rifle Corps, formerly The 60th.

The Duke of Edinburgh's (Wiltshire Regiment), 1st Batt., formerly
The 62nd; 2nd Batt., formerly The 99th.

The Manchester Regiment, 1st Batt., formerly the 63rd (West Suffolk); 2nd Batt., formerly The 96th.

The Prince of Wales's (North Staffordshire Regiment), 1st Batt.,
formerly The 64th (2nd Staffordshire); 2nd Batt., formerly The
98th.

The York and Lancaster Regiment, 1st Batt., formerly The 65th
(2nd Yorkshire, North Riding); 2nd Batt., formerly The 84th
(York and Lancaster).

The Durham Light Infantry, 1st Batt. formerly The 68th; 2nd
Batt., formerly 106th (Bombay Light Infantry).

The Highland Light Infantry, 1st Batt., formerly The 71st; 2nd
Batt. formerly The 74th.

The Seaforth Highlanders (Ross-shire Buffs, The Duke of Albany's
Own Regiment of Foot), 1st Batt., formerly The 72nd; 2nd
Batt., The 78th.

The Gordon Highlanders, 1st Batt., formerly The 75th (Stirling-
shire), 2nd Batt., formerly The 92nd.

The Queen's Own Cameron Highlanders, 1st Batt., formerly The 79th.

The Royal Irish Rifles, 1st Batt., formerly The 83rd (County Dublin); 2nd Batt., formerly The 86th (Royal County Down).

Princess Victoria's (Royal Irish Fusiliers) 1st Batt., formerly The 87th; 2nd Batt., formerly The 89th.

The Connaught Rangers, 1st Batt., formerly The 88th, 2nd Batt., formerly The 94th.

The Princess Louise's (Argyll & Sutherland Highlanders), 1st Batt., formerly The 91st; 2nd Batt., formerly The 93rd.

The Prince of Wales's Leinster Regiment (Royal Canadians), 1st Batt., formerly The 100th (Prince of Wales's Royal (Canadian); 2nd Batt., formerly The 109th (Bombay Infantry).

The Royal Munster Fusiliers, 1st Batt., formerly The 101st (Royal Bengal Fusiliers); 2nd Batt., formerly The 104th (Bengal Fusiliers).

The Royal Dublin Fusiliers, 1st Batt., formerly The 102nd (Royal Madras Fusiliers); 2nd Batt., The 103rd (Royal Bombay Fusiliers).

The Rifle Brigade (Prince Consort's Own).

The West India Regiment, 1st Batt., formerly Malcolm's Black Rangers; 2nd Batt., formerly The St. Vincent's Black Rangers.

The Royal Marines, Royal Marine Artillery, Royal Marine Light Infantry.

Q

TICONDEROGA

Ticonderoga, familiar as the name of the historic fortress at Lake George, was written by Sir William Johnson, in 1756, Tionderogue and Ticonderoro, and in grant of lands in 1760, "near the fort at Ticonderoga." Gov. Colden wrote Ticontarogen, and an Iroquoian sachem is credited with Decariaderoga. Interpretations are almost as numerous as orthographies. The most generally quoted is from Spofford's Gazetter: "Ticonderoga, from Tsin-drosie, or Cheonderoga, signifying 'brawling water,' and the French name, Carillon, signifying 'a chime of bells,' were both suggested by the rapids upon the outlet of Lake George." The French name may have been so suggested, but neither Tsindrosie or Cheonderoga means "brawling water." The latter is probably an orthography of Teonderoga. Ticonderoga as now written, is from Te or Ti, "dual," two; Kaniatare, "lake," and -ogen, "intervallum, divisionem" (Bruyas), the combination meaning, literally "Between two lakes." Horatio Hale wrote me of one of the forms "Dekariaderage, in modern orothography, Tekaniataroken, from which Ticonderoga, means, simple 'Between two lakes.' It is derived from Tioken, 'between,' and Kaniatara, 'lake.' Its composition illustrates a peculiar idiom of the Iroquoian language. Tioken when combined with a noun, is split in two, so to speak, and the noun inserted. Thus in combining Tioken with Oneonte, 'mountain,' we have Ti-ononte-oken, 'Between two mountains,' which was the name of one of the Mohawk castles—sometimes written Theonondioga. In like manner, Kaniatare, 'lake,' thus compounded, yields Te-kaniatare-oken, 'Between two lakes.' In the Huron dialect Kiniatare is contracted to Yontare or Ontare, from which, with io or iyo, 'great,' we get Ontario (pronounced Ontareeyo), 'Great lake,' which combined with Tioken, becomes Tionteroken, which would seem to be the original of Colden's Ticonderoga."

("Indian Geographical Names," by E. M. Ruttenber, page 71 Vol. VI, New York State Historical Association).

R

TESTIMONIALS TO THE BLACK WATCH.

The Virginia Gazette, July 30, 1767, published an article from which the following extracts have been taken:

"Last Sunday evening, the Royal Highland Regiment embarked from Philadelphia for Ireland, which regiment, since its arrival in America, had been distinguished for having undergone most amazing fatigues, made long and frequent marches through an unhospitable country, bearing excessive heat and severe cold with alacrity and cheerfulness, frequently encamping in deep snow, such as those who inhabit the interior parts of this province do not see, and which only those who inhabit the most northern parts of Europe can have any Idea of, continually exposed in camp and on their marches to the alarms of a savage enemy, who, in all their attempts, were forced to fly. * * * And, in a particular manner, the free-men of this and the neighboring provinces have most sincerely to thank them for that resolution and bravery with which they, under Colonel Boquet, and a small number of Royal Americans, defeated the enemy, and ensured to us peace and security from a savage foe; and, along with our blessings for these benefits, they have our thanks for that decorum in behavior which they maintained during their stay in this city, giving an example that the most amiable behavior in civil life is no way inconsistent with the character of the good soldier; and for their loyalty, fidelity, and orderly behavior, they have every wish of the people for health, honor, and a pleasant voyage."

Extract from speech by the elder Pitt in vindication of the employment of Highland Regiments of which the Black Watch was the first raised of the eighty-six during the four wars between 1739 and 1815.

"I sought for merit wherever it was to be found; it is my boast that I was the first Minister who looked for it and found it in the mountains of the North. I called it forth and drew into your service a hardy and intrepid race of men, who, when left by your jealousy, became a prey to the artifice of your enemies, and had gone nigh to have overturned the State in the war before the last. These men in the last war were brought to combat on your side, they served with fidelity as they fought with valour, and conquered for you in every part of the world."

S

COPY OF ALL REFERENCES TO THE BLACK WATCH OF THE TICONDEROGA PERIOD TO BE FOUND IN THE ARCHIVES OF THE DOMINION OF CANADA AT OTTAWA.

I am indebted for this Memorandum to Arthur Doughty Litt. D., Archivist of the Dominion of Canada.

1758.
March 29,
New York.

Abercrombie to Haldimand (?) Plan of operations settled at Home. Southern Operations.

Corps, Blakeney's, Lord John Murray's &c.

B.6   p.35

1756.
New York.

M.204-2   p.397   Shirley to Fox

Just arrived from Albany Major Abercrombie and General Webb arrived one on the 25th of June and the other the next morning with great part of Otway's Regiment and with all the Highland Regiments, &c.

In a letter from Abercrombie to London dated Albany, 3d August, 1756.

Col. Schuyler's New Jersey Regiment and four North Carolina Companies are barely sufficient to Garrison Oswego and keep the communication open to Schenectady and there remains the 48th Regiment together with Otway's and the Highlanders to Garrison Fort William Henry, &c., &c.

M.205-1 p.

1756.
June 21.
New York.

James Abercrombie to——On the 15th of April sailed from Plymouth and arrived here on the 16th June with General Otway's and Lord John Murray's Regiments, &c.   B.205-1   p.8

LORD·HOWE STONE
Unearthed at Ticonderoga, Oct. 1889. Now Preserved at Headquarters
House

1756.   Loudon to Fox.
Aug. 29,
Albany.

Though I was informed that the whole Transports with the Highland Recruits were arrived, I
heard this morning that there were still five missing, and that those that are come were very short
of Provisions, they were victualled only for two
months, &c., &c.   M.205-1 p.240

1756.   Shirley to Loudon.
Sept. 4.
Boston.

Upon this I beg leave to observe to your Lordship, that it appearing from Col. Webb's letter to
me dated from New York the 9th June, that Otway's and the Highland Regiments might be daily
expected there (Oswego).

What confirms me in the matter is, that your
Lordship told me, when I had the honour to wait
on you, when the day you set from New York, being the 26th July that the Garrison at Oswego was
so weak, that the 44th Regiment was to be sent to
strengthen it and at the same time your Lordship
mentioned, that you thought 900 men, by which I
suppose your Lordship meant Otway's and the
Highland Regiments were but a few to cover the
country.

                                         M.205-2 p.306

1756.   Loudon to Fox
Nov. 22,
Albany.

The 42nd Regiment, I quarter at Schenectady,
from whence they take the posts, on the Mohawk
river, &c.

                                         M.207-1 p.2

1757.
April 25.
New York.

Loudon to Pitt.....................:..............................

As the Garrison (Fort Henry) had been troubled with the scurvy I had ordered Lieutenant General Otway's Regiment to relieve them, and Colonel Monro met the account of the attack being made on the Fort on his march; he immediately left his baggage, and made all possible dispatch to Fort Edward, where he received the account of their being retired. Colonel Gage and Burton followed him directly with the remains of the 44th and 46th Regiments and the Highlanders were set in motion from Schenectady. They all marched without Tents, and lay in the woods, &c.

We have on that river (Mohawk), at Schenectady, and up to the German Flats, the Highland Regiment, upwards of a thousand men, &c.

M.207-1 p.174

1758.
Feb'y 14.
New York.

Loudon to Pitt...

....storming of Fort Herkemer and I threw in part of the 42nd Regiment of Highlanders into Schenectady, that there might be no want of numbers for this service.   M.208. p.2

Divisions of Manuscripts,
    February 22, 1911.

T

THE BLACK WATCH MEMORIAL AT TICONDEROGA.

The genesis of this memorial was an address made by the late Joseph Cook at the services held in front of the boulder erected to the heroes of Ticonderoga, Academy Park, Ticonderoga, N. Y. July 31, 1899, in which he made this remark: "There ought to be a memorial to the Black Watch composed largely of Scotch Highlanders who, with the Colonials charged Montcalm's entrenchments for eight consecutive hours."

Major D. L. Wilson Farguharson, D. S. O., at "Allargue"

Representation of the Black Watch at Unveiling of Memorial Tablet,
Ticonderoga, July 4, 1906

The writer, who was secretary of the Ticonderoga Historical Society at that time, had the honor of being the medium through which this chance remark became an enduring memorial of brick and stone. He was unsuccessful, however, until Mr. David Williams, the publisher of "The Iron Age," a summer resident of Ticonderoga at Rogers Rock, came to his assistance. Mr. Andrew Carnegie was the generous donor of the funds to build this memorial. The grants were in two amounts, the first gift for a public library with the usual provisions, and the second gift, with no limitations, with which to build an historical addition to the library, thus makng it both a public library and historical building.

The laying of the corner stone, Oct. 4, 1905, was made the occasion for one of the greatest celebrations Ticonderoga has ever seen. The pipe band of the 5th Royal Scots of Canada, Highlanders, now the 5th Royal Highlanders of Canada, from Montreal, and the Regimental band and a Battalion of the 5th Infantry, U. S. A., from Plattsburgh, were the principal features of the parade. It was particularly appropriate that the Royal Scots should be present, as they are allied to the Black Watch and wear the same uniform. It was also an education to the thousands of spectators, few, if any of whom had ever seen Highlanders in full regimentals marching to the music of bagpipes. After the exercises of the day, the Royal Scots visited the ruins of old Fort Ticonderoga, about two miles from the village and the picture of a body of Highlanders with their scarlet coats and tartan kilts marching up the green slopes of the old ramparts, with the setting sun behind them, was one never to be forgotten and which probably had not occurred since the Revolution.

The officers of the present Black Watch Regiment, then stationed at Fort George Scotland, being advised of the Memorial sent the following letter to the secretary of the Ticonderoga Historical Society:

"Dear Sir: Your letter 9th Sept., 1905, on the subject of a Black Watch Memorial, has been perused by the Commanding Officer and the Officers of the 1st battalion of The Black Watch, formerly called the 42nd Royal Highland Regiment, and it was also submitted and discussed at the Annual Gathering of Black Watch

Officers—past and present—recently held in Edinburgh. I am authorized to inform you that all Ranks of the Regiment are proud to know that the Ticonderoga Historical Society had decided to appropriate an alcove in the Ticonderoga Free Public Library as a memorial to the 42nd Regiment, to commemorate their services in the engagement before Fort Ticonderoga on July 8, 1758. The suggestion contained in your letter, to the effect that Officers of the Regiment might be disposed to erect a tablet on a wall of the Alcove to the memory of the officers and men of the 42nd who were killed or wounded in the action has met with the unanimous approval of those to whose notice it has been brought, and I am to inform you that such a Tablet will gladly be provided and that the work of executing the Tablet will be entrusted to a London firm as soon as a suitable design has been decided upon. In order to assist us in choosing a suitable form of tablet I shall be much obliged if you can favor me with a rough plan of the alcove, the dimensions of the actual wall on which the Tablet will rest, and an idea of the general style of the building.

I shall be glad to hear from you as soon as you can conveniently supply the information for which I have asked.

I am, Sir, yours truly,

D. L. Wilson Farquharson,
Major The Black Watch.

The exercises for the unveiling of the memorial tablet July 4, 1906, was made the occasion for another grand celebration at which the full bag pipe band of the 5th Royal Highlanders of Canada and a company of 50 men from the same regiment, making a total of 75 Highlanders, were a feature of the parade. Major D. L. Wilson Farquharson of the Black Watch, came over from Scotland to unveil the tablet in behalf of the Regiment. It was accepted by Frank B. Wickes of Ticonderoga for the Ticonderoga Historical Society. The address of the day was delivered by Senator Edgar T. Brackett of Saratoga Springs.

—Photo by L. Def. Cone, Ticonderoga

THE BLACK WATCH MEMORIAL AT TICONDEROGA

Two views of the 5th Royal Highlanders of Canada who attended ceremonies of laying corner stone and of unveiling Memorial Tablet

List of Officers, Non-Commissioned Officers and Partial List of Men Composing Ticonderoga Detachment, 5th Royal Highlanders of Canada, July 4th, 1906.

Capt. A. F. Gault.
Capt. V. C. Buchanan.
Capt. C. M. Monsarrat.
Capt. J. Muir, Quartermaster.
Sergt. Major D. A. Bethune.
Q. M. Sergt. B. Howard.
Col. Sergt. J. H. A. Mackay.
Staff Sergt. T. A. Gardiner.
Staff Sergt. J. Phillips.
Sergt. C. Denman.
Sergt. P. Forde.
Sergt. T. Mitchell.
Bugle Sergt. P. Broadhurst.
Drum Sergt. F. W. Flood.
Drum Major, G. Foley.
Pipe Major, D. Manson.
Sergt. J. MacLean.
Corp. P. W. MacFarlane.
Corp. H. Massey.
Corp. N. Manson.
Corp. P. Sutton.

Privates.

J. Bayley.
F. H. Benson.
Walsh.
A. E. Smith.
S. Tapster.
Scobie.
P. Roache.
J. Cockburn.
A. Bishop.

J. A. McLean.
Jeffries.
W. Marsh.
J. Ferguson.
J. Corbett.
J. Palmer.
C. Myers.
C. Black.
J. Stuart.
J. Roney.
Dean.
A. Reid.
A. Williams.
A. Betts.
D. Reid.
L. Pickering.

Pipers.

R. Morrison.
M. McLeod.
J. Ferrier.
D. McArthur.
D. Brash.
J. Husband.
B. Milligan.

Drummers.

J. Ryan.
Gore.
Kemp.
Jones.

Printed in December 2022
by Rotomail Italia S.p.A., Vignate (MI) - Italy